Shakespeare's History Plays
The Family and the State

Shakespeare's History Plays

THE FAMILY AND THE STATE

Robert B. Pierce

OHIO STATE UNIVERSITY PRESS

Library of Congress Catalogue Card Number 73-157047
Standard Book Number 8142-0152-0
Manufactured in the United States of America

To my mother, Edna B. Pierce

Table of Contents

Preface

I HAVE tried to avoid two pitfalls in the following study, one of pursuing a hobbyhorse at the expense of Shakespeare's plays and the other of bogging down in the conflict whether or not the history plays embody Tudor orthodoxy. On the first of these, I have chosen to write about the theme of the family because it seems important in the plays and because it cuts across the normal critical lines between language, characterization, plot, and theme. I have studied the relationship of the family to the political themes of the history plays, thus isolating one significant part of Shakespeare's dramatic craft and of his development during the 1590s. (I have omitted *Henry VIII* from my study because it comes so much later and is significantly different in theme and dramatic technique.) I have tried to keep my subject clearly in mind lest the discussion lose focus and become impressionistic commentary on the plays in general. At the same time I have avoided quoting every occurrence of the word "father" and have sought to relate the dramatic significance of the family to a broader view of the plays.

PREFACE

Seeing Shakespeare's histories as orthodox is no longer itself orthodox, as perhaps it was during the first years after John Dover Wilson's *The Fortunes of Falstaff* and, above all, E. M. W. Tillyard's *Shakespeare's History Plays*. Since I share much of Tillyard's view in particular, I seem to be open to the standard charge of "turning the plays into moral homilies." Let me protest now that I do not see the purpose of the plays as inculcating anything. They hold the mirror up to nature, a quite sufficient task for any drama. They do not *teach* that political order is a good thing nor that wives should obey their husbands, though they do *assume* these truisms of Renaissance orthodoxy in much the same way as they assume that kindness is better than cruelty. Although the argument has gotten very complex—in particular, because of that useful term *ambiguity*—many recent critics want us to see a Shakespeare who is bitterly pessimistic about the course of history and who sternly disapproves of the strong rulers among his characters, especially Henry V as both prince and king. The first of these views seems to me truer than the second, though even there I detect no modern-style existential anguish behind the grim portrayal of a century of "carnal, bloody, and unnatural acts."

At any rate, my critical purpose is to study a dramatic motif, not to contribute directly to this ongoing argument. I refer to specific points at issue only where other critical readings seem to me to distort the dramatic significance of the family. In one way, however, my study is relevant to the central issue. Many critics make use of a familiar distinction between public and private virtues, granting the former but not the latter to Prince Hal, for example. If the family is an important motif in the way I describe it, that seems to be a powerful argument against such dualism, at least in any simple form. Still, my first concern is to show that the motif of the family is present and important; only secondarily do I try to make political and moral inferences from it.

Since I do not see the eight history plays on the fifteenth century as an epic cycle in Tillyard's sense, I have avoided searching for subtle links among them. Clearly they are not autonomous entities in the same way as *Macbeth* and *King Lear;* in particular, the Henry VI plays and the Henry IV plays have a close connection among themselves. Still, each was presumably written to be played alone on one afternoon and therefore to a different audience from even its nearest companion. Hence it is rash to make too much of such conceivable parallels as that between Hotspur's marriage and Henry V's. Shakespeare's language calls for some recollection of earlier historical plays in the later ones, especially of *Richard II* in the Henry IV plays, but I seldom go beyond the connections that he specifically makes.

There is no solution to the problems of documenting other criticism of Shakespeare. I have tried to indicate some at least of my major sources by footnotes, though the absence of any reference indicates neither my unfamiliarity with a critic nor my dismissal of him; and a disagreement on detail may be my only reference to someone who has taught me much. I have no doubt failed to read many fine studies and have misunderstood others; I can only hope that these errors have not seriously weakened my conclusions and that the paucity of footnotes has discreetly veiled my ignorance.

By no means all of my obligations are to printed sources. I am especially grateful to Herschel Baker, who sponsored and guided the doctoral dissertation out of which this book comes; to Alfred Harbage, who also read it at that stage; to David Young, who has since provided encouragement and intelligent advice; and to Oberlin College for a grant that allowed me to dredge many a learned quotation from sermons and courtesy books in that Mecca of scholars, the British Museum. Quotations from Shakespeare are from the admirable New Arden texts when they are available. For *Richard III*, which is not yet published in that series, I have used the original Arden edition. Part of Chapter VI has appeared in a slightly different form as "The Generations in *2 Henry IV*," *Twentieth Century Interpretations of Henry IV, Part Two*, ed. David P. Young (Englewood Cliffs, N.J., 1968), pp. 49-57.

Shakespeare's History Plays
The Family and the State

*The good prince ought to have
the same attitude toward
his subjects, as a good
paterfamilias toward his
household—for what else
is a kingdom but a great
family? What is the king
if not the father to a
great multitude?—Erasmus,*

*The Education of a
Christian Prince*

Chapter I

IF man stands at the center of drama, in Shakespeare's history plays it is public man, man as ruler, courtier, warrior, or citizen. We may see love and friendship and the intimacies of private life, but they are secondary to a panoramic view of public events. The reign of King John and the civil wars of the fifteenth century come to dramatic life in all their turbulence and suffering in the nine history plays that Shakespeare wrote just at the end of the sixteenth century. Implicit in the events and explicit in the speeches of the characters are some of the timeless issues of public life. A humanist in at least this broadest sense as he deals with history, Shakespeare seeks guidance for the present in the events of the past. Yet he is first of all a dramatist; unlike the historian Edward Hall and the poet Edmund Spenser, he is inclined to dramatize the events and issues without drawing an explicit moral.[1] In short, his plays are not didactic, but they are political drama. They have a richly varied interest, but central to them is a contrast between order and wise government on the one hand and disorder and war on the other.

3

It is hardly surprising that even in such plays men have a private existence as well as a public one. Kings are sons and husbands like other men, and courtiers fall in love or quarrel with their brothers even while they share in the rise and fall of nations. But family life plays an especially prominent role in the language, characterization, and dramatic structure of these plays. Indeed, frequent references to the family help to define the issues shown on a national scale in the public world. At times the family becomes a miniature of the kingdom, and its life provides direct or ironic comment on the life of the commonwealth. My purpose is to study how Shakespeare develops this analogic relationship between family and state in ever richer and subtler ways through the nine history plays of the 1590s.

The Elizabethan family was not identical to our contemporary institution. For one thing, it was a larger group with more varied bonds among the members; in that sense it was already closer to the public realm, less autonomous. The great noble families were one of the main political institutions of the world that Shakespeare dramatizes in the history plays. Even the individual household was a broad group including several generations and sometimes other members without blood ties, such as apprentices or pages. Most Renaissance moralists follow Aristotle in counting the servants as part of the family. Another difference is that childhood did not yet have the distinctive role and value that we give to it. Also, especially in the noble houses, personal relations often seem to have been more formal and less intimate than in the modern middle-class fam-

4

ily. Still, human feelings change less than social forms; the drama of family relationships in Shakespeare is surprisingly open to our intuitive apprehension even while we have to make some allowances for historical alteration.

No doubt moral theorists of the Renaissance make the ideal family sound more different than was the reality, but their ideas on the family and the state can be useful to us as readers and viewers of the history plays, especially because Shakespeare could assume considerable familiarity with these ideas in his audience. Erasmus's quotation at the head of this chapter is a common sentiment in Elizabethan writing, both learned and popular; and it suggests one basic difference between Shakespeare's day and ours. What sounds to us like a mere figure of speech has metaphysical reality for Erasmus. In the divinely governed order of nature, the king is to the commonwealth as the father is to the family, the sun in the sky, the lion among animals, the eagle among birds, and so on. Omens demonstrate the reality of this symbolic order. In *Macbeth* an owl kills a falcon, which is above it in the hierarchy of birds, shortly before Macbeth kills his king. God made the world a living organism in which one part affects the other by mysterious ways, and He also made it a book to be read by man. The wise man understands the present and even sees hints of the future by studying these correspondences, as E. M. W. Tillyard calls such patterned relationships.[2] One of the most commonly observed correspondences in the Renaissance is that between the family and the state. Though Shakespeare's handling quickly develops beyond the conventions of his age, the comparison is for him not a private symbol but a publicly recognized mode of thought.

What parts of family life do Renaissance thinkers associate with the state? What lessons do they draw? Fortunately there is little difference on these matters. Catholics and Protestants may differ on the relative merits of single and wedded life and on the proper grounds for divorce, but the clergy who write moral essays on the family, the writers of courtesy books, and the countless pedagogues who prescribe a suitable education for princes and nobles all find about the same political lessons in the family, lessons that often derive from Aristotle and Cicero. In a much-paraphrased description, Cicero sums up a whole body of thought about the home: "This is the foundation of civil government, the nursery, as it were, of the state."[3] Thomas Pickering develops the idea in a typical way: "Upon this condition of the Familie, being the Seminarie of all other Societies, it followeth, that the holie and righteous government thereof, is a direct meane for the good ordering, both of Church and Commonwealth."[4]

Such a connection between the family and the state is all the easier because in Renaissance handbooks the science of government is typically a study of individual virtues applied to public questions. When they prescribe an education for kings and magistrates, writers like Erasmus and Sir Thomas Elyot base their discussions on the four cardinal virtues.[5] A good king is simply a good man on a heroic scale. Machiavelli, who seemed to deny this truism of the age, was anathema. If James I is typical, kings themselves proclaimed the orthodox view. His book of advice to his son derives a moral lesson from the history of his own family: "Haue the King my grand-fathers example before your eies, who by his adulterie, bred the wracke of his lawfull daughter & heire; in begetting that bastard, who vnnaturally rebelled, & procured the ruine of his owne Souerane & sister."[6] Such moralizing on his grandfather's grave may sound priggish to our ears, but that kind of priggishness is frequent in Renaissance homilies.

Books like William Perkins's *Christian Oeconomie* concentrate on three family relationships: husband and wife (including courtship), parent and child, and master and servant. Texts aimed at a more aristocratic audience often show awareness of the broader family group, the noble house; but all writers focus on husband and wife and parent and child when they make connections with the state. A husband should rule over his wife like reason over the passions or the mind over the body; Stefano Guazzo puts it into political terms: "And as men oughte to observe and keepe the lawes and statutes of the countrey: so women ought to fulfill the commaundements of their husbandes."[7] But women are not to be completely servile. Pierre de la Primaudaye echoes a popular sentiment (ultimately from Aristotle's *Politics*) that a man should be to his wife like the government of "a popular state," to his children like a king.[8]

The relationship that fascinates these writers is the tie between father and son. Typically the mother is less significant, simply a bad influence of varying degrees of importance. Not only is the son the father's immortality, but he is also the moral inheritor of the family tradition. The whole idea of nobility rests on the assumption that men inherit at least an inclination toward virtue or vice.[9] Henry Peacham is completely orthodox: "As for the most part, wee see the children of Noble Personages to beare the lineaments and resemblance of their Parents: so in like manner, for the most part, they possesse their vertues and Noble dispositions, which even in their tenderest yeeres will bud forth, and discover it selfe."[10] Even the tutors, with their vested interest in the claims of nurture, make an important place for nature.

The imagery of planting and growing is a constant vehicle of this doctrine, one that Shakespeare often uses. Annibale Romei pronounces the inheritance of virtue in typical form: "In a manner it alwayes falleth out, that in armes, and vertuous actions, the most singular and excellent men, be of nobility: For Nature hath inserted a certaine secret vertue, in the seede of all things, which giueth them force and property, to be like the beginning, from whence they are deriued."[11] If noble birth signifies potential virtue, bastardy as a violation of natural order implies moral degeneration. The moralists hesitate to damn all bastards, but Thomas Becon suggests that most do sooner or later go wrong.[12] And at least on the Elizabethan stage they normally live up to their reputation.

Moral inheritance is a special bond between the family and the state because it is central to the theory of royal succession. In Shakespeare as in the chroniclers, one major link in the chain that leads to the Wars of the Roses is Bolingbroke's seizure of the throne, displacing Richard II's rightful line. For orthodox thinkers

nature itself demands that kings inherit by primogeni-
ture, and that is so because the new king naturally inherits his father's heroic virtue. Even the most idealistic
knew that such was not always the case, and Shakespeare makes quiet irony of the fact that the son whom
Henry V and Katherine compound for will be no con-
queror of the Turk but the weak Henry VI. Still, the
full irony depends on our consciousness of the doctrine.
Like the theorists of moral inheritance, poetic Platonists
knew that beautiful women are not always virtuous.
Such facts are signs of a degenerate world; ideally,
according to nature, a fair skin means a beautiful soul,
and a heroic king engenders a heroic prince. Hence the
welfare of the kingdom itself rests on the king as a
father. Erasmus, that most sensible of idealists, points
the moral by adding nurture to nature: "It is a great
and glorious thing to rule an empire well, but none-
the-less glorious to pass it on to no worse a ruler: nay,
rather it is the main task of a good prince to see that
he [the son] does not become a bad one."[13]

These ideas about the family and the state pervade
the writing of the time and so provide a public basis
for Shakespeare's art. He need not imply acceptance
of these principles: if Edmund in *King Lear* illustrates
the degeneracy of the bastard, Faulconbridge in *King
John* inverts the commonplace with equally striking
dramatic effect. Shakespeare's audience is prepared to
see connections between the family and the state and
hence to perceive one kind of dramatic structure in the
history plays.

Still the possibility of such connections does not define the kind of plays Shakespeare will write, nor does

it solve all the dramatic problems. His history plays are much more complex and sophisticated in their handling of political ideas than those of other Elizabethan writers,[14] but the ideas that characters talk about are those of the popular treatises, not those of Machiavelli, Guicciardini, and Bacon with their subtle analysis of statecraft. The plays themselves share this concern with broader, more easily accessible issues. Even if one is inclined to find Tillyard's picture of a cycle on the Tudor myth too tidy, there is no disputing his emphasis on the theme of order and succession. Whereas it would be narrowing to say that *King Lear* is about wisdom through suffering or any other one phrase, it is more accurate to say that the Henry VI plays are about disorder in the state.

The unifying vision of all nine plays is of an ideal state bound by majesty, as Max M. Reese calls it,[15] and epitomized by England under Henry V. Contrasted with that vision is the terrible reality of England in civil war. Such a theme might suggest a general, rather impersonal drama, what in fact we see in *Gorboduc*. That play focuses on the public side of men, on the ruler and his advisers. The medieval dramatic themes of man's fall and redemption are more personal, more expressive of the whole being of the characters, than the theme of order and succession in the state.

In the pattern of political drama that *Gorboduc* illustrates, certain kinds of material are less congenial than others. Its severe balances of character and event and above all its rigidly formal rhetoric are appropriate to characters conceived of in their public roles, as political and ethical types. With this kind of high cere-

monial technique, Henry V can meet the French am-
bassadors, but Hal in the tavern is a problem. The
audience can respond to a kingly declamation on ideo-
logical and patriotic grounds, but they know their taverns intimately and personally. A Shakespeare who
wrote high moral tales in his histories would seek techniques to subdue the private sides of his characters to
an overriding public tone. Actually, however, Shakespeare appeals to the whole range of response in his
public audience, including the familiar and personal.
He must devise techniques for maintaining public
language and themes in harmony with a more intimate
realism than *Gorboduc* can afford.

The dramatic problem is especially acute in scenes
involving family relationships, which raise to a new
level of complexity the issue of realism in characterization. A character in a play seems realistic to the extent
that he evokes attitudes and emotions that we would
feel toward such a man in real life, whereas a stylized
character evokes a narrow range of responses. We know
all that we need to know about the stylized figure
Talbot in *1 Henry VI* when we see that he is the English hero. The nature of our response is set to the extent
that we are, at least imaginatively, good English patri-
ots. Although Prince Hal is also the English hero, he is
a far more complicated dramatic figure. His characterization is more realistic than Talbot's, not because
his motivation is clearer, but because he shows more
sides of the complex reality that we perceive in men.

The same alternatives are possible with the family.
Talbot and son embody a family relationship, father
and son; but what we see of them is only one element

in the rich complex of emotional bonds possible: chivalric loyalty to each other. Hal too displays such loyalty to his father in the battle at Shrewsbury, but the emotional drama is complicated. He dislikes and shuns the court; his father misunderstands his nature even while grasping their estrangement with full human feeling. Thus a family relationship can be as stylized or as realistic as an individual character. Shakespeare's dramatic problem is to maintain a thematic focus on the public issues of Tudor political theory without deadening the family by turning it into just an emblem. As the question poses itself even in the earlier, simpler plays, can he make dramatic capital of Henry VI as a henpecked husband while showing him as a well-intentioned but weak king?

Almost inevitably the solution of this technical problem implies an attitude toward the role of the personal in public affairs. Is it true, as Derek Traversi argues, that a Shakespearian hero's political success forces him to sacrifice his full humanity, that part of Hal must die before Henry V can reign?[16] Or is the opposite true; is the family "the school of those sentiments of loyalty and kindness which must be extended into other human relationships if organized society is to exist"?[17]

Recent study of medieval and Renaissance dramatic tradition has greatly enriched and complicated our understanding of the variety of forms available to Shakespeare at the end of the sixteenth century, but it is still useful in looking at the history play to contrast the influences of classical tragedy and medieval drama. In the classical tradition the plays of Seneca and his Renaissance followers offer a model for serious drama about public figures.[18] The Senecan tradition—severe, formal, and rhetorical—provides a rigid structure for the most flamboyant matter, a useful quality for Elizabethan playwrights. Also, Seneca shapes his plays around a small, clear body of ideas not totally different from the concerns of Shakespeare's histories. Finally, the Senecan form can be reconciled with much of the morality form, the severest side of the native tradition, as the fusion of the two in *Gorboduc* shows.

In an age that was seeking models for literary form, Seneca must have been a more imposing figure than he can be today. Reinforced by similar elements in Ovid's poetry, Seneca's lurid tragedies were one major influence on the developing tragedies and history plays of the 1580s and 1590s.[19] In particular they offered a collection of melodramatic horrors along with a means of keeping them under dramatic control. Curiously enough, given his bloody themes, Seneca is the most impersonal of playwrights, a moralist contemplating depravity from the stoic heights. His abstractly rhetorical language depersonalizes his characters into models of various ethical conditions. Hence their sufferings are not so horrible as to shock us into unbelief. Seneca's ethical themes endure this process of abstraction well since his ethic is based on a highly theoretical view of human nature.

To develop this ethic, he groups his characters in two equally artificial types, the same figure sometimes vacillating between the two. One type includes men so overcome by passion—usually love, hatred, or revenge—that their actions are wildly irrational. Such a figure can be the tyrant-villain, like Nero in *Octavia*,[20] a favorite pattern for the Renaissance Senecans. The other and rarer type is the stoic, austere in controlling his passions and full of good advice. Both kinds of character are little more than abstract embodiments of Seneca's ideas. If for one moment Atreus and Thyestes were real, *Thyestes* would be an intolerable and therefore incredible horror. The artistic success of the play (and it is a minor one) is to govern the melodrama of its fable by its stern impersonality.

Like their Greek models, Seneca's tragedies are based on conflict within the family, and the Greek plays demonstrate how deep the emotional intensity of such themes can be. Seneca, however, is at his most rigidly impersonal in dealing with family relations. He uses the lofty rank of his characters to justify their public, almost oratorical quality. His aristocrats live in a special dramatic world like the moral world that Clytemnestra claims for them: "lex alia solio est, alia privato in toro" ["There is one law for thrones, one for the private bed"].[21]

The Senecan rhetoric that delighted the Renaissance can be sheer poetic exuberance, but it is also a means of distancing the characters, keeping them from too familiar a reality. In the dying Hercules' words to his mother, Seneca earns a splendid rhetorical force with understated irony: "Herculem spectas quidem, / mater" ["Hercules thou seest indeed, my mother"].[22] It is interesting to see how the personal tone of John Studley's Tudor English version shatters the decorum: "I am your Hercles mother deere."[23] In an attempt to arouse pathos, Studley brings his Hercules too close to ordinary men.

Even the *Troades,* more pathetic than most of Seneca, is in this lofty vein. The fine irony of Hecuba's
bitter reaction to the deaths of Polyxena and Astyanax
is epigrammatic:

> concidit virgo ac puer;
> bellum peractum est.

[A maiden and a boy have fallen; the war is done.][24]

As the general nouns indicate, the specific identities
of the maiden and boy are unimportant in the power
of this figure. Violation of family ties is the greatest
of Seneca's melodramatic horrors, but his impersonal
method typically relies on the labels of family relationship for a generalized pathos. When Medea kills her
children, it is mother stabbing child, not individuals,
because the audience knows nothing of the children
and she herself is a rhetorical passion more than a
woman.

The whole movement of Senecan rhetoric is toward
abstract ideas rather than toward the personal. The
broken fraternal bond of Thyestes and Atreus suggests,
not pathos or ironic images of happy domestic life, but
epic images of the cosmos shattered when family ties
break. When Thyestes looks on the severed heads of
his sons, he laments with cosmic scope:

> sustines tantum nefas
> gestare, Tellus? non ad infernam Styga
> tenebrasque mergis rupta et ingenti via
> ad chaos inane regna cum rege abripis?

[Canst thou endure, O Earth, to bear a crime so monstrous?

Why dost not burst asunder and plunge thee down to the infernal Stygian shades and, by a huge opening to void chaos, snatch this kingdom with its king away?][25]

In its language *Gorboduc* is a worthy imitator of Seneca's scope and abstract vision, though it lacks his compactness and melodramatic vigor. More than the Renaissance Senecans, Shakespeare can recapture this style when he wants to, as parts of *Richard III* show with splendid energy.

If the Roman dramatists were an important influence on Elizabethan drama, still its parentage lies rather in the native tradition. John Ruskin describes Gothic naturalism with its emphasis on the concrete and particular as central to medieval art, but that is only one side of the truth. The medieval drama is a vehicle for Christian ideas, especially the central theme of man's fall and redemption. If the Tudor descendants drift away from these themes, the more serious among them turn rather to secular morality than to pure storytelling. Both medieval and Tudor dramas use a number of the same commonplaces as Seneca, his "small coin of philosophy."[26] Senecan maxims constantly note the futility of ambition and the omnipotence of Fortune. As a result of this similarity of purpose, the unreal, the stylized, the typical are denizens of the medieval theater too; but they are curiously mixed with a more familiar reality. As a brilliant discussion by Erich Auerbach contends, the Christian tradition of combining sublimity and humility justifies a mixture of styles in order to domesticate theological truth.[27] Characters like Everyman and Mankind are abstractly conceived, but

16

their speech combines sententiousness with the language of ordinary men facing ordinary problems. Everyman's cousin refuses to join him in his journey to Death, not with an elaborate show of theological sophistry or libertine philosophy, but because he claims to have a cramp in his toe. Such language and details bring theological truth close to the domestic experience of the audience.

The popular audience found something that they liked and wanted more of in the comic or realistic language and details that colored their religious drama. When they watched *Mankind,* one mood responded dutifully to the high sentences of Mercy, while another delighted in the irreverent interruptions of Mischief. He relied on what they knew, not lofty reasoning and aureate phrases, but plain English country life: "Corn seruit bredibus, chaff horsibus, straw fyrybusque."[28] Indeed, the courtly and scholarly audience was not too proud for such indecorum; the French Senecans could not have produced *Gammer Gurton's Needle.*

The fragile decorum of Seneca's drama would collapse at such brushes with the familiar, and the English playwright's problem is to avoid such a catastrophe. The double structure of the *Second Shepherds' Play* involves one kind of solution to that problem, parodic contrast. Mak's wife and the stolen sheep are a grotesque parallel to the Virgin and Child, but the distorted echo suggests both the imperfection of the fleshly world in which we dwell and its dim connection with the Divine, at that moment completing the link by the miracle of the Incarnation. Not blasphemous laughter but comic awe is the final tone as the humble

17

shepherds come to Christ's birth with their gifts of cherries, bird, and ball. Perhaps because the Christian theme of Incarnation embodies a full conception of humanity, it can survive this contact with the familiar and personal.

If realistic comedy can be combined with ritualism and solemn morality, so can domestic pathos. In *The Sacrifice of Isaac* the suffering of Abraham and the naïve fears of his son are touching even while they embody one of the great theological mysteries. Later drama is not always so skillful. John Bale does not dare to trust his Kynge Johan and the militant Protestant code that he embodies under the clear light of realistic language, and so he turns such language and familiar details to account in satirizing the evil Popish schemers. Here, as in *Mankind,* the effect is to split the play into serious-heroic and comic-familiar parts with little organic connection between the two. From such origins come the cruder forms of Elizabethan comic relief.

Not all the early Tudor plays are so divided, however. John Phillip's *The Play of Patient Grissell,*[29] registered for publication in 1565/66, applies the techniques of the Tudor interlude to one of the great medieval stories (most familiar in Chaucer's version, the *Clerk's Tale*). This story comments on the themes of marriage and the relationship between the aristocracy and the lower classes. Despite his nobles' reluctance, Walter, a marquis, chooses a lowborn bride named Grissell. During their marriage he tests her submissiveness, spurred on in his tests by a Vice figure called Politic Persuasion, who recites the commonplaces of jocular medieval antifeminism. By manifesting the patience that has made her name proverbial, Grissell wins back her children and her husband's trust along with the full loyalty of the nobles.

An overlay of classical learning does not conceal the fundamental morality structure of the play with its episodic plotting, stylized handling of time and place, Vice figure, and emblematic characters like the courtiers Fidence, Reason, and Sobriety. In her "symple Smocke" Grissell is the vehicle of a great deal of lofty preaching, yet there is no split between the didacticism of the play and its immediacy. Its merits are on the whole those of the genre and the story; Phillip is not an especially able craftsman; but he demonstrates that, in developing a family theme, a playwright can unite realism and a lofty moral tone.

One group of plays is especially significant in showing the potentialities of a family theme. During the early Tudor period, dramatic representations of the Prodigal Son story became widely popular.[30] This story fitted naturally into the medieval tradition of the Psychomachia, and an older classical influence than the Senecan also helped to develop it. The northern humanists had developed a school drama patterned on Terence, of which one example was the Dutch William de Volder's *Acolastus*, acted in 1528.[31] With considerable ingenuity the play adapts the parable of the Prodigal Son to Terentian form with a primarily didactic purpose. Pelargus, the father, has a wise friend and counselor named Eubulus, and Acolastus, the son, an evil counselor named Philautus. Acolastus, taught by Philautus to ignore his father's good advice and even the Bible given to him, leaves home for the sinful city of Rome. There he falls into the toils of two parasites and a courtesan, the three of them closely imitated from Latin comedy. Stripped of his money and clothes, Acolastus sinks lower and lower until, when his father prays for him, he feels a mysterious infusion of grace and returns to his father's joyful reception. With a timid piling-up of negatives, a "Peroratio" asserts that the play has allegorical import:

> Nolo putes spectator optime, hic nihil
> Mysterij latere tectum, ludicra
> Sub actione. (p. 179)

[I do not want you to think, noble spectator, that there is no mystery here, hidden under the comic action.]

The play is more ingenious than inspired, but it was immediately popular, going through some twenty editions by 1540, the year in which John Palsgrave translated it into English. Such English counterparts as *Nice Wanton, The Disobedient Child,* and *Misogonus* soon appeared in England.

The theme of the Prodigal Son has at least three potential dramatic interests. First there is the secular morality on the temptations of youth, which earlier plays like *The Interlude of Youth* and *Wit and Science* also represent. In the Tudor interlude this level is not inconsistent with another, a vigorously realistic exploration of the taverns and brothels where the youth is tempted and falls. But finally, behind this story, there always lurks the potentiality of its original meaning, the straying of the soul from God the Father and its return. The extent to which the story is secularized can be marked by the extent to which the Prodigal's father loses this overtone and becomes a Latin-comedy father. In *Acolastus,* for example, both sides are there, albeit in awkward juxtaposition. The father is too much of a fool to carry the allegorical weight De Volder wants to give him. This awkwardness may explain the apologetic tone with which the "Peroratio" announces the "hidden" allegory.

In Thomas Ingelend's *The Disobedient Child,* [32] published about 1560 and perhaps written a decade earlier, the father has lost most of this allegorical overtone. Designated only as "The Rich Man," he is even more a fool than Pelargus until his son's follies teach him wisdom. When the son, now tied to a shrewish wife, comes home repentant, his father pities him and gives him money but tells him that he must endure his lot. This turn may represent a sterner, more Calvinistic theology, but only at the expense of obscuring the original meaning of the parable. The traditional happy ending can be varied because the son is no longer a figure for mankind or even youth, a development that reflects the growing particularity of the genre.

Although *The Disobedient Child* is a bookish and homiletic play, it shows the way for a much livelier example of the genre. *Misogonus* was probably written in the 1560s or 1570s.[33] Philogonus, the father, is quite foolishly human, though still interminably didactic; and Misogonus, the corrupted son, is involved in some of the most vigorous tavern scenes of the tradition. The author adds a new element, an Italianate romance plot with a long-lost elder brother. (The elder brother of the parable had dropped out of many of the earlier versions, but now he reappears in this odd transformation.) As one might expect, the varied elements of this play do not entirely mesh. Although the text is incomplete, it is hard to imagine how the missing last act could attain any greater harmony, whether Misogonus's repentance in Act IV lasts or not.

George Gascoigne's *The Glass of Government,* published in 1575, and *Eastward Ho,* a joint production of Chapman, Jonson, and Marston published in 1605, represent later variants of the tradition, which is humorously glanced at by *Histrio-Mastix,* performed in 1599, as well as by Falstaff. In time the Prodigal Son is again lost in the witty youth of Latin comedy, as in the impecunious rake of Stuart and Restoration drama; but this process is slow and irregular, as even this brief survey has suggested. It will be necessary to ask what levels are being exploited when Shakespeare alludes to the Prodigal Son theme, as he does most importantly in the Henry IV plays. In addition, this popular genre shows how other playwrights were coming to terms with some of the problems that Shakespeare faced in the history plays.

If Shakespeare can be thought of as primarily in the native tradition, then he must have felt called on to include the details of familiar life that his audience had come to expect, the tavern scenes and the "symple Smockes." That is at least the simplest explanation for those ingratiating bits of Elizabethan local color in *The Comedy of Errors,* the most classical of his plays. But Plautus and Terence are more easily reconciled to this technique than Seneca because of their low style and domestic plots, as relatively successful combinations like *Jack Juggler* and especially *Gammer Gurton's Needle* illustrate. Serious drama takes up the public stories of kings and princes, who (except for an occasional Prince Hal) do not normally frequent taverns and brothels, nor does the loss of a needle exercise them greatly. However, they do have families; that is one point of contact with the everyday lives of their audience. None of the men in the audience had lost a kingdom like Henry VI, but presumably many of them had shrewish wives. Whether Shakespeare could afford to exploit this potentiality of his themes or whether he had to veil the family of his kings and nobles in Senecan impersonality remains to be explored.

It would be possible to use the doctrine of correspondences as a source of references to the family in a very impersonal way. Since the family is a mirror of the state, events in the one can symbolize those in the other. An example of this device in *Gorboduc* parallels Shakespeare's early use of the family. Toward the end of the play, in piling up the misfortunes that come from disorder in the state, Eubulus laments:

> The father shall vnwitting slay the sonne;
> The sonne shall slay the sire, and know it not.[34]

Shakespeare expands the idea of these lines into a dramatic exemplum of the chaos in the state when in *3 Henry VI* the ineffectually saint-like king watches the battle of Towton. As he looks on, the stage direction explains: "Alarum. Enter a Son that hath kill'd his Father, at one door; and a Father that hath kill'd his Son, at another door" (II.v.54).

Here the family is introduced to a political play and subordinated to the political theme. As in Seneca, the appeal is to the labels of family life, to father and son in general rather than to concrete individuals. The language of the characters, rigidly stylized, culminates in an almost operatic lament by the son, father, and King Henry. Verisimilitude is deliberately banished in order to focus attention on the thematic significance. Shakespeare uses the family as a correspondence, direct or ironic, all through the history plays. There are extended scenes like this one or the parallel scene of Aumerle's treason and his father York's denunciation of him in *Richard II,* and there are single poetic figures like the Gardener's simile in that play:

> Go, bind thou up young dangling apricocks,
> Which like unruly children make their sire
> Stoop with oppression of their prodigal weight.[35]

Within this emblematic technique Shakespeare can dramatize some of the most important political issues of his plays. Indeed, many dramatists of the 1590s and earlier use the family in this way. Perhaps the most obvious device is making the family a microcosmic parallel to the disorder of the state or an ironic contrast. Rebellion is the same principle whether it operates in the state or in other parts of the social fabric. Hence the *Homily Against Disobedience and Wilful Rebellion* argues:

> For he that nameth rebellion, nameth not a singular or one only sin, as is theft, robbery, murder, and such like;

but he nameth the whole puddle and sink of all sins against God and man, against his prince, his countrymen, his parents, his children, his kinfolks, his friends, and against all men universally.[36]

Conversely, family disorder embodies the same evil as political rebellion.

One sees this technique entering the drama when *Respublica* (1553) allegorizes the imperiled commonwealth as a gullible widow. In that curious adaptation of Seneca to English political purposes, Thomas Hughes's *The Misfortunes of Arthur* (1587/88), political disorder is constantly expressed by disorder in the family. Thus Cador vows to fight in support of Arthur:

> Were it to goare with Pike my fathers breast,
> Were it to riue and cleaue my brothers head,
> Were it to teare peecemeale my dearest childe.[37]

The spectacle of intrafamilial warfare between Arthur and Mordred supports these rhetorical figures. Obviously, such a technique is useful for melodramatic intensification, but it can also yield quieter effects. In *The Massacre at Paris,* as Harry Levin points out, the fact that the Guise is cuckolded demonstrates his isolation and hidden weakness.[38]

Another idea of central importance is moral inheritance. A man's role in the state is determined by his birth, and he learns how to assume that role through his blood and the example of his ancestors. To argue this doctrine in *The Book of the Courtier*, Castiglione uses the stock metaphor of inheritance as a plant growing from its seed: "Because nature in every thing hath depely sowed that privie sede, which geveth a certain force and propertie of her beginning, unto whatsoever springeth of it, and maketh it lyke unto her selfe."[39] It is typical that, even while imitating Marlowe's Tamburlaine, Robert Greene makes his Alphonsus in *The Comical Historie of Alphonsus King of Aragon* son of the rightful heir to the throne. Thus the hero's *virtù* is given roots in a noble heritage. *The Raigne of King Edward the Third*, one of the Shakespeare apocrypha, goes more deeply into the process of moral inheritance than most of the other non-Shakespearian history plays. We see the Black Prince emulating the heroic virtue of his father, and he proclaims his victory as a pattern for future generations:

> Now, father, this petition Edward makes
> To thee, whose grace hath bin his strongest shield,
> That, as thy pleasure chose me for the man
> To be the instrument to shew thy power,
> So thou wilt grant that many princes more,
> Bred and brought vp within that little Isle,
> May still be famous for lyke victories![40]

Finally, dramatists exploit an old and very natural technique in measuring a political event by its impact on the family. The Homilies constantly argue that rebellion disrupts the whole order of the state and hence the welfare of the family. Rebellion will lead "the brother to seek, and often to work the death of his brother; the son of the father, the father to seek or procure the death of his son, being at man's age."[41]

Another attack on rebellion gives a picture of disorder that foreshadows the speech of Ulysses in *Troilus and Cressida*:

> Take away kings, princes, rulers, magistrates, judges, and such estates of God's order, no man shall ride or go by the high way unrobbed, no man shall sleep in his own house or bed unkilled, no man shall keep his wife, children, and possession in quietness, all things shall be common; and there must needs follow all mischief and utter destruction both of souls, bodies, goods, and commonwealths.[42]

The device has obvious theatrical possibilities. Cambises shows his tyranny by killing a boy before his father's eyes in Thomas Preston's lurid tragedy. (The incident is a stock exemplum among the moralists and pedagogues.) At greater length, in the two parts of *King Edward the Fourth,* Thomas Heywood shows how a king's weakness can put a citizen in an impossible dilemma of loyalties: When his wife becomes mistress to one king and hence an object of the next king's anger, Matthew Shore can neither reject her nor take her back. Hence he must refuse her offer to give up the king and return to virtue. To save her from adultery is to be a traitor.[43]

Thus in many Elizabethan plays the family is an emblem of larger issues in the state. The technique is apparent all through Shakespeare's history plays. If that is their only use of the family, then clearly the handling is in the Senecan tradition, Seneca Elizabethanized by an elaborately figurative and imagistic style and perhaps reinforced by the abstractions of the moralities, but unchanged in his rigid impersonality. In this emblematic habit there is nothing of the native drama's appeal to familiarity and realism. That would only distract the kind of attention necessary.

Manifestly, however, there is another side of the matter. In *King John* there may be something symbolic about Faulconbridge's bastardy and his vigorous affirmation of descent from Richard the Lion-hearted, but there is nothing abstract and metaphorical about his characterization. In the councils of kings and nobles he bluntly utters what the Englishman in the audience would like to say. He is in one part of his nature the essence of common sense. Faulconbridge is a successful characterization above all because of this appeal to familiar qualities, not because of his abstract symbolic meaning. Is it possible to combine these two modes of handling a character, or does the one necessarily counteract the other, so that common sense demands omitting any metaphorical significance in Faulconbridge's birth? Samuel L. Bethell's theory of multiconsciousness suggests that the Elizabethan audience was able to respond to different levels of meaning at the same time.[44] Hence we need not assume that only one of the traditions can be functioning.

I shall discuss Shakespeare's history plays in their approximate order of composition (the precise order is a vexed problem) so as to observe their developing skill in relating the family and the state. There are figures and analogies based on the family and relying on the Elizabethan habit of seeing correspondences. There are scenes of family life injected into the middle of historical events but more or less distinct from them, like those of Hotspur and his wife. Finally, there are passages and even whole plays in which the family is inextricably mixed with the political situation through characters portrayed both in their public roles and as members of their families. Henry IV and Hal are king and heir-apparent, but they are also father and son, with all the potentialities of that relationship for dramatic development.

One cannot study Shakespeare's craftsmanship in any detail without taking into account the significance of the plays. The distinction between structure and theme is a slippery one, since the theme of a play gives it one kind of structure. Thus in *contemptus mundi* tragedy, the theme of man's dominance by the Wheel of Fortune gives schematic form to the plot. This form is used even by such comparatively advanced plays as *The Book of Sir Thomas More.* Even more popular in Elizabethan drama is the cycle of crime and punishment motivated by revenge, which gives pattern to *Richard III* as well as many lesser plays. Use of such schematic themes as a formal pattern need not imply the author's intellectual commitment to them as descriptions of reality, and so easy generalizations about Shakespeare's growing political wisdom as reflected in the later history plays are dangerous. The didactic passages in *1* and *2 Henry IV* are not notably wiser than those in the Henry VI plays. To what extent the more complex structure of the later history plays represents philosophical growth and to what extent it is more subtle craftsmanship, or whether the craft of imitating life is much the same as the wisdom to understand it: these are not easy questions to decide. At any rate, the two sides—the ideas and the craft—must be studied together.

Finally, I cannot discuss the technique and function of references to the family without considering the kind of response that an Elizabethan audience might have given, and this consideration involves the traditions on which Shakespeare draws. Such traditions are agreements (in part, unconscious) between the writer and his audience that the writer will order certain kinds of material certain ways in order to command a special kind of attention from the audience. Much writing in recent years has described how Shakespeare and other dramatists allude to the morality figure of the Vice in some of their characterizations and so evoke a special range of responses in their audience beyond the potentialities of naturalistic drama. John Dover Wilson among others has found the same kind of significance in Falstaff's ancestry.[45] I shall need to discuss what potentialities of the classical and native traditions Shakespeare uses in his handling of the family. All of this is only one small part of his drama, but if it offers a microcosm of his development in technical skill and the ability to give form to a meaningful vision of life, then it is surely worth detailed study.

---

[1] For a more consistently didactic and topical reading than mine, see Lily B. Campbell, *Shakespeare's "Histories": Mirrors of Elizabethan Policy*, 3d ed. (San Marino, Calif., 1963). For a judicious study of topical elements in drama from late medieval times to 1603, see David Bevington, *Tudor Drama and Politics* (Cambridge, Mass., 1968).

INTRODUCTION

[2] *The Elizabethan World Picture* (London, 1950), especially chaps. vi and vii.

[3] *De Officiis,* trans. Walter Miller, Loeb Classical Library (New York, 1923), p. 57.

[4] Dedication to his translation of William Perkins, *Christian Oeconomie* (London, 1609), fol. 3ʳ.

[5] See the introduction to Lester K. Born's edition of *The Education of a Christian Prince* (New York, 1936) and his article, "The Perfect Prince: A Study in Thirteenth- and Fourteenth-Century Ideals," *Speculum* 3(1928), 470-504, for discussion of the origins and early growth of this literature.

[6] *The Basilicon Doron of King James VI,* ed. James Craigie, Scottish Text Society, 3d ser. (London, 1944), XVI, 133.

[7] *The Civile Conversation of M. Steeven Guazzo,* trans. George Pettie and Bartholomew Young, Tudor Translations, 2d ser. (New York, 1925), VIII, 30.

[8] *The French Academie,* trans. T. B. (London, 1586), p. 531. The idea comes from Aristotle, *Politics* I.12.

[9] See Ruth Kelso, *The Doctrine of the English Gentleman in the Sixteenth Century* (Urbana, Ill., 1929), p. 23.

[10] *Peacham's Compleat Gentleman,* ed. G. S. Gordon (Oxford, Eng., 1906), p. 14.

[11] *The Courtiers Academie,* trans. John Kepers (London, 1598), p. 231.

[12] "The Booke of Matrimony," *The Worckes of Thomas Becon* (London, 1564), I, fol. 652ʳ and 652ᵛ.

[13] *The Education of a Christian Prince,* p. 141.

[14] Notable exceptions include Marlowe's *Edward II* and the play called *Woodstock: A Moral History* in the edition by A. P. Rossiter (London, 1946).

[15] *The Cease of Majesty: A Study of Shakespeare's History Plays* (London. 1961), p. vii.

[16] *Shakespeare from Richard II to Henry V* (London, 1957).

[17] Alfred Harbage, *Shakespeare and the Rival Traditions* (New York, 1952), p. 297.

[18] Although this discussion implies more influence from Seneca than Howard Baker would admit, his pointing to Ovid as an alternative influence is an important corrective. In style, in characterization, and in some of the specific maxims and turns of phrase, the early Shakespeare is at least as much Ovidian as Senecan, though the two modes are often hard to distinguish. Likewise the medieval influences Baker

31

points to are themselves partly Ovidian and Senecan. See *Induction to Tragedy* (Baton Rouge, 1939).

[19] One cannot precisely distinguish Shakespeare's contribution from that of other writers, since little is known about the early development of the history play. The texts are few, often bad, and difficult to date. At any rate, Shakespeare's second tetralogy carries the genre far beyond what the other extant plays offer.

[20] *Octavia* may not be by the author of the other tragedies, but most Renaissance readers attributed them all to Seneca. It is in the Senecan pattern and has influenced Elizabethan drama like the others. Also it is a kind of history play, though not a useful model to Shakespeare in its way of narrating complex events.

[21] *Agamemnon*, l. 264. Both Latin and English versions of Seneca are from *Seneca's Tragedies*, ed. Frank J. Miller, Loeb Classical Library, 2 vols. (New York, 1916-17).

[22] *Hercules Oetaeus*, ll. 1345-46

[23] *Seneca His Tenne Tragedies Translated into English*, ed. Thomas Newton (New York, 1927), II, 238.

[24] *Troades*, ll. 1166-67.

[25] *Thyestes*, ll. 1006-9.

[26] John W. Cunliffe, *The Influence of Seneca on Elizabethan Tragedy* (London, 1893), p. 23.

[27] Of a passage in the twelfth-century *Mystère d'Adam*, he writes: "The episode which is here presented to us in dramatic form is the starting point of the Christian drama of redemption, and hence is a subject of the utmost importance and the utmost sublimity from the point of view of the author and his audience. However, the presentation aims to be popular. The ancient and sublime occurrence is to become immediate and present; it is to be a current event which could happen any time, which every listener can imagine and is familiar with; it is to strike deep roots in the mind and the emotions of any random French contemporary" (*Mimesis: The Representation of Reality in Western Literature*, trans. Willard Trask [Garden City, N.Y., 1957], p. 131).

[28] Line 57. Quoted from *Chief Pre-Shakespearean Dramas*, ed. Joseph Quincy Adams (Boston, 1924), p. 305.

[29] Ed. R. B. McKerrow and W. W. Greg, Malone Society Reprints (London, 1909).

[30] There is a concise history of the genre in Felix E. Schelling, *Elizabethan Drama 1558-1642* (Boston, 1908), I, 63-66.

[31] *The Comedy of Acolastus*, ed. P. L. Carver, Early English Text

INTRODUCTION

Society (London, 1937). The introduction and notes are a massive source of information about this play and its influence.

[32] *The Dramatic Writings of Richard Wever and Thomas Ingelend,* ed. John S. Farmer (London, 1905), pp. 43-92.

[33] "A Mery and Pleasaunt Comedie Called Misogonus," *Quellen des Weltlichen Dramas in England vor Shakespeare,* ed. Alois L. Brandl (Strassburg, 1898), pp. 419-89.

[34] V.ii.213-14. Quoted from *Chief Pre-Shakespearean Dramas.* Shakespeare need not have known this passage, since a phrase in Hall could have given the clue from which he developed the scene in *3 Henry VI* (if a clue was necessary). For the quotation from Hall, see H. C. Hart's note on the stage direction at II.v.54, *The Third Part of King Henry the Sixth,* Arden Edition (London, 1910). The stage direction in the text is quoted from Hart, who substantially follows the First Folio.

[35] The last line seems to imply the Prodigal Son theme, though not very importantly here.

[36] *Certain Sermons or Homilies Appointed to Be Read in Churches* (Oxford, 1822), p. 524 (hereafter cited as *Homilies*).

[37] III.iii.77-79. Quoted from *Early English Classical Tragedies,* ed. John W. Cunliffe (Oxford, Eng., 1912).

[38] *The Overreacher: A Study of Christopher Marlowe* (Cambridge, Mass., 1952), p. 85.

[39] Trans. Sir Thomas Hoby, The Tudor Translations (London, 1900), XXIII, 44-45.

[40] V.i.216-22. Quoted from *The Shakespeare Apocrypha,* ed. C. F. Tucker Brooke (Oxford, Eng., 1918). The language hints at another correspondence, that with God the Father and Christ.

[41] "The Third Part of the Homily Against Disobedience and Wilful Rebellion," Second Book, *Homilies,* p. 529.

[42] "An Exhortation Concerning Good Order and Obedience to Rulers and Magistrates," First Book, *Homilies,* p. 105.

[43] See "The First Part of King Edward the Fourth," *The Dramatic Works of Thomas Heywood* (London, 1874), I, 84.

[44] "A popular audience, uncontaminated by abstract and tendentious dramatic theory, will attend to several diverse aspects of a situation, simultaneously yet without confusion" (*Shakespeare and the Popular Dramatic Tradition* [New York, 1944], p. 28).

[45] *The Fortunes of Falstaff* (New York, 1944).

33

Chapter II

THE HENRY VI PLAYS

BEFORE E. M. W. Tillyard's influential study of the histories appeared in 1944, critics generally looked on the Henry VI trio as formless chronicle plays. H. B. Charlton's dismissal is typical: "The whole matter of *Henry VI* has no dramatic form. There is no dominant interest, recognizable as a dramatic interest, to hold the audience in continuous suspense."[1] A criticism directed toward character analysis almost inevitably reaches such a conclusion, but by turning to theme, Tillyard finds a substantial unity in the whole first tetralogy. He emphasizes its awareness of moral causation in history and especially its concern with the nature of political disorder.[2] Tudor Englishmen remembered with horror the Wars of the Roses. Given such an audience, Shakespeare has seized on the most immediately meaningful part of England's history and turned it into a great pageant on the moral causes and consequences of political disorder. The dramatic technique changes and in part develops from play to play, but the theme is simple and continuous.

The family in the Henry VI trilogy has no independent role; it is not a conflicting center of interest that competes with the political theme for attention. Rather it functions almost entirely as a commentary on the causes and consequences of political disorder. For the most part these characters are not torn between their personal and political identities as Henry IV is; the same force cripples them in both realms. "Though violent, they are, in a deeper sense, all strangely passive: they are at the mercy of circumstances and their uncontrolled selves."[3] What is most real in the plays is historical destiny, to which the personal identities of the characters are subdued.

Reference to the family is often a device to bring their political roles closer to the immediate experience of the audience. We understand Henry as king because we understand him as father and husband. We know what is happening to England because we see what is happening to fathers and sons and husbands and wives. This pattern reflects the doctrine of correspondences. Since what infects the kingdom infects everything in it, marriage becomes just another part of the struggle for power and loved ones are hostages to fortune in a violent world. The very channels that perpetuate order are corrupted to breed disorder. Inheritance, turned to a monstrous thing that demands vengeance rather than noble emulation, finally produces a demon who is the enemy of both family and state.

Shakespeare also uses the family to suggest what political disorder is destroying in the commonwealth. Especially in the first two plays glimpses of a yet-uncorrupted family life contrast ironically with the decline of justice and harmony among the governors.

This contrast does not suggest that personal virtue conflicts with political virtue—quite the opposite, though in some degree Henry VI's piety cripples his political realism. Still there may be some hint that his early piety does not run very deep.[4] Certainly his asceticism vanishes quickly at Suffolk's descriptions of Margaret in *1 Henry VI*. And in adversity Henry gains a real political wisdom, while at the same time his piety becomes more convincing. Better than anyone else in *3 Henry VI*, he understands the plight of England, including the threat of Richard, Duke of Gloucester; and he foresees England's redemption by the young Richmond. More serious weaknesses than unworldly piety cripple Henry both as king and as husband and father. The key to his character is that he is a partial man and a partial monarch.

More typical of these plays is the illusory personal loyalty of the York family. It quickly collapses because, in a realm where no strong king commands unexceptionable loyalty, every man is tempted to struggle for himself, even against his brothers. Thus one remarkable achievement of the Henry VI plays is the way that they marshal the powerful claims of family loyalty in defense of political order. Above all they show that the family is involved in the destructive impact of disorder. Partly for this reason, they are significant achievements in dramatic craftsmanship. It is no disparagement of Shakespeare's youthful talents to attribute them to his pen.

1 Henry VI

Despite Charlton's dismissal, the bones of structure

are, if anything, too prominent in the first of the Henry VI plays. Most obvious is the parallel between disorder in the English court and collapse in the French wars. The opposing powers of order and chaos appear concretely in the contrast between the ideal Talbot and the demonic Joan of Arc. Their careers, and indeed all of the chronicle history, suffer free distortion to make a political fable. As H. T. Price describes the process, "Shakespeare is imposing upon a body of historical data a controlling idea, an idea that constructs the play."[5] Though one may allow for hyperbole when R. W. Chambers finds an Aeschylean power in *1 Henry VI*,[6] the play is often quite impressive in embodying the theme of disorder, and part of this impressiveness comes from its use of the family.

Disintegrationists of the text, those who attribute parts to different authors, find their best ammunition in its undistinguished language. Its abrupt shifts from workaday verse to the extremes of Senecan rant prevent any coherence of tone. The family is present in the language, though not in great enough density to be a unifying leitmotiv. For example, there is a traditional use of correspondence in the description of Humphrey, Duke of Gloucester, as "a father to the commonweal" (III.i.98). The servingman who thus invokes the Renaissance doctrine of natural order goes on to show how political disorder is involving even ordinary men and their families:

> We and our wives and children all will fight
> And have our bodies slaughter'd by thy foes.
> (III.i.100-101)

THE HENRY VI PLAYS

With rhetorical extravagance Bedford predicts universal disorder, foreseeing a time

> When at their mothers' moist eyes babes shall suck,
> Our isle be made a nourish of salt tears,
> And none but women left to wail the dead.
> (I.i.49-51)

Joan of Arc employs an image of suffering motherhood to sway the wavering Burgundy with the plight of France:

> As looks the mother on her lowly babe
> When death doth close his tender dying eyes,
> See, see the pining malady of France.
> (III.iii.47-49)

Thus Shakespeare uses family images to emphasize, directly and by contrast, the wide and terrible impact of political disorder and war.

Birth and inheritance are prominent in the language of the play. The interview between York and his dying uncle, Mortimer, brings out one of the central political issues of the play, the doubtfulness of the king's title. Here and elsewhere the favorite metaphor for orderly succession is growth, especially a flourishing tree or garden. Any interruption of the pattern—depicted as cutting down or transplanting—perverts a natural process. One inherits not only his position but also his virtue and social responsibility. When Joan charges Burgundy with an unnatural betrayal of his country, she goes on to question his "birth and lawful progeny [lineage or descent]" (III.iii.61). When Talbot strips Falstaff[7] of his Garter, he denounces the recreant as a "hedge-born swain" despite his pretensions to good blood (IV.i.43). Here the embodiment of virtue and order, whose son shortly demonstrates the proper inheritance of valor, describes his opposite.

The theme of birth and inheritance is dramatized in the emblematic Temple Garden scene (II.iv), where the conflict of Lancaster and York emerges in association with the metaphor of red and white roses. The episode gains power by combining an emblematic method with vividly realistic portrayal of the angry quarrelers. The witty play with the roses is natural enough in the mouths of these young law students and courtiers, and Shakespeare differentiates their dramatic voices with skill and economy. The precise nature of the quarrel is unclear, but it quickly brings up the issue of York's birth. Using the pervasive image of plants and growth, Warwick appeals to his friend's parentage as a sign of his nobility: "Spring crestless yeomen from so deep a root?" (85). Somerset replies that York has inherited corruption rather than nobility because of his father's treason.

There is no hint of York's claim to the throne, though presumably his father was guilty unless their title is valid. Already, however, there is an unconscious irony in his boast that he will wear the white rose

> Until it wither with me to my grave,
> Or flourish to the height of my degree.
>
> (110-11)

His relation to degree is ambiguous. Is he the rightful sovereign needed to restore order to England, or is his ambition the enemy to degree, the weed that the Gardener in *Richard II* says must be cut down? The ambiguity of York's inheritance is an early hint of how orderly succession becomes more and more perverted and monstrous in the tainted world of Henry VI's England. When in the next scene York takes up his dying uncle's claim to the throne, he finds both glory and destruction for himself and his family.

In the Temple Garden scene the dominant symbol is the garden itself with its red and white roses. This symbol embodies one side of the family motif, the cluster of traditional ideas involving birth and inheritance. The issues of family inheritance are fundamentally the same as those of succession in the monarchy, and so the two are linked in this scene as they will be throughout Shakespeare. In Act IV he returns to the emblematic method in a group of scenes between Talbot and his son, and there the relationship of father and son is the symbol used to provide a commentary on political disorder. However, these scenes are the thematic center of a whole development in the play, the contrast between Talbot and Joan of Arc. In that context their meaning will be more readily apparent.

Talbot is an earlier and simpler version of the warrior-hero Henry V. Neither of these men makes any pretense to super-humanity like Tamburlaine's. They find their strength where a weakling like Richard II finds despair, in their ordinary human nature. Whether the hero-king woos Katherine in bluff English fashion or wanders incognito through the night to meet his soldiers as one of them, he grounds his royalty in the earth. Nor is Talbot the stock image of a hero; Shakespeare even changes his sources to make the terror of the French physically dwarfish.[8] There are times when he speaks with the stereotyped rant of heroes and behaves with unrealistic bravado. Thus he brags that, while a prisoner, he refused to be exchanged for an unworthy opposite. But his behavior in captivity shows an almost animal ferocity rather than heroic dignity:

> Then broke I from the officers that led me,
> And with my nails digg'd stones out of the ground
> To hurl at the beholders of my shame.
>
> (I.iv.43-45)

The extremes of behavior thus crudely juxtaposed are more subtly fused in Henry V, but the Shakespearian impulse to ground the hero in something more solid than epic glory is already present.

Talbot's self-discipline and virtue appear primarily in his military feats, but on two occasions he is measured by more personal values. The first of these is a light interlude in the French wars, the Countess of Auvergne's attempt to trap him by inviting him to an assignation. Talbot reveals a Guyon-like continence when he brings his army along to the dinner. His domestic virtue resists French seductiveness as strongly as his courage resists French arms. The connection of this episode with Talbot's heroic career is tenuous, but for that very reason Shakespeare's intention of measuring the private virtue of a public figure is apparent.[9]

This episode is most important in preparing the way for the more effective scenes in which Talbot and his son fight and die together near Bordeaux (IV.v-vii). Here most clearly Shakespeare uses the values of the family to complete the ideal portrait of Talbot and to provide an ironic contrast with the disorder and disloyalty of the court. This relationship of father and son symbolizes the kind of political order that is dying along with Talbot. When he calls young John "the son of chivalry" (vi.29), he means "my chivalric son," but the loose Elizabethan grammar allows the phrase to suggest that chivalry is an inherited virtue, a mark of the noble family.

Young Talbot's refusal to abandon his father proves that he has inherited that heroic warrior's zeal for honor. His argument against flight is unanswerable:

> The world will say, he is not Talbot's blood
> That basely fled when noble Talbot stood.
>
> (v.16-17)

Talbot endorses this traditional doctrine when he reports having taunted the Bastard Orleans:

> Contaminated, base,
> And misbegotten blood I spill of thine,
> Mean and right poor, for that pure blood of mine
> Which thou didst force from Talbot, my brave boy.
>
> (vi.21-24)[10]

In the dying chivalric order, not only does the father's blood infuse strength and virtue into the veins of his son, but the effect of breeding is reinforced by example, a kind of emulation in courage. Hence Talbot's son inspires him to new deeds of valor, and John demands parity with his father even while affirming their unity:

> No more can I be sever'd from your side
> Than can yourself yourself in twain divide.
>
> (v.48-49)

The destruction of this family foreshadows the collapse of the state, for at King Henry's court the old order has already degenerated into bastard feudalism, a disorderly society of Machiavellian scheming veiled by remnants of the old ceremony.

The special style of these scenes is characteristic of the early Shakespeare's emblematic method. Tillyard brands it "the conventional, the formal, the stylised"[11] and considers it an inadequate way to heighten the effect of Talbot's death. However, the studied artificiality of the verse has another function, to direct attention toward the symbolic weight of the scenes. The poetic idiom is determinedly classical with its stichomythy, its formidable regularity, and its rhetorical pointedness. The classical warrior-hero appears (with Renaissance heightening) in Talbot's description of his son fighting over him "like a hungry lion" and then sallying forth in a rage at the enemy's retreat (vii.5-13). The verse technique is in some ways parallel to the ritualism of the moralities, but it is closest to Ovid, Seneca, and the neo-Senecan plays like Gascoigne and Kinwelmershe's *Jocasta*. In a similar episode of that play, Creon and his son Meneceus

44

debate whether the latter should be sacrificed for Thebes. A bit of their stichomythy will illustrate the likeness:

> *Cre.* If such a death bring glorie, give it me.
> *Mene.* Not you, but me, the heavens cal to die.
> *Cre.* We be but one in flesh and body both.
> *Mene.* I father ought, so ought not you, to die.[12]

Shakespeare adds rhyme to increase the pointedness and tightens the rhetorical structure, but the scenes are alike in their formality and sententiousness.

For this final episode Talbot's animal ferocity is absent so that he and his son may be abstract patterns of English heroism. As in Seneca, the appeal of the verse is to general labels rather than vividly imagined particulars, to "blood," "mother," "name," and "fame." This movement toward abstraction reaches cosmic scope in Talbot's speech at the close of Scene v with its astronomical quibble on "son":

> Then here I take my leave of thee, fair son,
> Born to eclipse thy life this afternoon.
> Come, side by side, together live and die,
> And soul with soul from France to heaven fly.
>
> (52-55)

The Ovidian myth of Daedalus and Icarus is rather arbitrarily brought in at vi.54-55, reiterated at vii.16, and then ingeniously transcended in an image suggestive of heroic apotheosis:

> Coupled in bonds of perpetuity,

Two Talbots winged through the lither sky,
In thy [Death's] despite shall scape mortality.
(vii.20-22)

Shakespeare cultivates this heightened and artificial
language in order to give the Talbots' loyalty symbolic
weight. The scenes gain power by incremental repetition, not only of words and phrases, but also of images
and ideas. Hence the repetitiousness that leads John
Dover Wilson to suspect dual authorship[13] is more
probably a literary device, albeit one largely alien to
modern sensibilities.

Perhaps the finest effect of the episode is the ironic
contrast produced by an abrupt shift of tone when the
French enter to vaunt over the heroes' dead bodies.
Typical of their blunt, prosaic comments is the misbegotten Orleans's reference to "the young whelp of
Talbot's" (vii.35). But it is Joan, Talbot's demonic
foe, who points the contrast in tone when she undercuts Lucy's pompous recital of the dead warrior's
honors:

Him that thou magnifiest with all these titles,
Stinking and fly-blown lies here at our feet.
(vii.75-76)

Her practical directness counterpoints the artificiality
of the previous scenes and thus enforces their significance: in this degenerate world the ideal embodied by
the Talbots is dead.

Joan is Talbot's "mighty opposite," the epitome of
disorder and rebellion just as he is the epitome of

order and loyalty. They share a blunt directness of speech that gives them force in this world of empty rhetoric and aimless plotting. Talbot would not be ashamed to choose his sword like Joan, "Out of a great deal of old iron"; after all, he was willing to fight his captors with stones. But he would not have the blasphemous audacity to attribute the choice to divine guidance (I.ii.98-101). Like Richard III, Joan arouses her creator's interest, not because of any goodness in her, but because she has a real zest for evil. She is absolutely corrupt from beginning to end, a degeneracy shown in part by her violation of familial sanctions.

Most obvious are the constant references to her sexual libertinism. The innuendos start when she first appears, and later she is openly the Dauphin's paramour. In ironic proximity to Talbot's victory over temptation by the Countess of Auvergne, Burgundy describes having seen "the Dauphin and his trull" in undignified flight together (II.ii.28). Her corruption is yet more obvious when she offers her body to fiends, and she becomes ludicrous when she abandons her pose of virgin purity and proclaims herself with child in order to avoid execution. Allowing such a trull to stand boasting over the dead Talbot suggests the triumph of degeneracy. And even her death does not purge the world, because she is soon to be replaced by Queen Margaret, another Frenchwoman and one equally vicious though less contemptible.

Heavily symbolic of Joan's evil is a violation of family duty when at the point of death she repudiates her father. As France rebels against England's rightful dominion, so its champion denies her parentage. The half-comic scene is in a rude, blunt language appropriate to Joan and her father, yet through the coarse irony appears something of Shakespeare's usual compassion for the sufferings of old men. To an Elizabethan the stage picture of a daughter refusing to kneel for her father's blessing goes beyond comedy; it is a terrible image of disorder. In *The Life and Death of Lord Cromwell*, the hero shows his filial piety by kneeling to his blacksmith father just after being made Lord Chancellor. When Joan's father curses her, he shows what is all too rare in this play, an individual poetic voice; but the images are at the same time broadly evocative of disordered nature:

> Wilt thou not stoop? Now cursed be the time
> Of thy nativity! I would the milk
> Thy mother gave thee when thou suck'dst her breast
> Had been a little ratsbane for thy sake;
> Or else, when thou didst keep my lambs a-field,
> I wish some ravenous wolf had eaten thee.
> Dost thou deny thy father, cursed drab?
> O, burn her, burn her: hanging is too good.
>
> (V.iv.26-33)

Joan repudiates her father to claim gentle birth; she pretends to the inherited virtue that young Talbot epitomizes and York claims to embody. There is probably an ironic pun in her claim:

> No, misconceived Joan of Aire hath been
> A virgin from her tender infancy.
>
> (V.iv.49-50)[14]

48

She is not misunderstood but misbegotten, a monstrous example of base inheritance and pretension to rank. Hence Joan is the antithesis of Talbot, and their contrasting attitudes toward family values are one symbolic vehicle of the opposition.

While disposing of Joan, the last act (in the modern division) turns to a new theme, the king's marriage. Henry VI displays his weakness in all his acts, but nowhere more clearly than in his marriage. The relationship between Henry and Margaret develops through all three plays after its introduction at the end of *1 Henry VI*. There a few brief scenes contrast two attitudes toward marriage, one that supports order in the state and one that undermines it. Henry himself expresses the former (albeit protesting too much) when, after declaring his freedom from lustful desires, he says:

> I shall be well content with any choice
> Tends to God's glory and my country's weal.
>
> (V.i.26-27)

Since a king ought to marry according to his country's interests, Henry accepts Duke Humphrey's plan to salvage some of the French empire by a tactical marriage. He is duly contracted to the Earl of Armagnac's daughter. But even in this court of empty ceremonies there is something more than usually specious about the official professions of love; Henry V manages to fall convincingly in love with his Katherine even while being just as conscious of his interest as these negotiators. Nevertheless, a state marriage entails utilitarian

49

motives; Henry is submitting himself to the necessities of kingship.

The Duke of Suffolk, who introduces Henry to the second view of marriage, first comes to prominence when he captures Margaret only to fall victim to her beauty. This episode introduces the language of Petrarchan love to the play. As a private man Suffolk is permitted to indulge his love, or at least would be if he were single, but he infects the king with the same attitude in urging him to wed Margaret. When the Duke leads his pupil in love onstage, Henry is using the conventional Petrarchan love imagery of storms and ships himself (V.v.1-9). Suffolk's hint at sexual pleasure seems to shock the pious young king (16-21), but the Duke's casuistry soon persuades him to violate his previous contract.

There is dramatic irony in Suffolk's argument against marriages of state:

> For what is wedlock forced but a hell,
> An age of discord and continual strife?
> Whereas the contrary bringeth bliss,
> And is a pattern of celestial peace.
>
> (62-65)

Forced marriages are indeed condemned by all Renaissance moralists, but so are marriages for desire alone.[15] This marriage is a pattern, but a pattern of the discord that is overwhelming the English commonwealth. Margaret's masculine strength of will, which has only faintly appeared in the rather conventional battle of wits with Suffolk, assumes clearer form in an ominous reference to

> Her valiant courage and undaunted spirit,
> More than in women commonly is seen.
>
> (70-71)

Henry's domestic weakness, complemented by the unnatural presumption of his wife and her ambitious lover Suffolk, will help cause the Wars of the Roses. Even now it is only the strong will and benevolence of Gloucester, the Protector, that prevent the onset of civil war.

Conclusion.—Thus the family is significant in the structure of *1 Henry VI*. Its system of values provides a standard to measure the disorder and moral nihilism that are infecting England and even beginning to corrupt the domestic lives of the rulers. What prevents this dramatic technique from having more than occasional flashes of power is that Shakespeare's exploitation of it lacks immediacy. "The theme . . . is England, and the characters are drawn firmly, but as political, not private, figures. Private, realistic touches do indeed break through the political formalism and rhetoric, but they are few."[16] In the scene between Joan and her father the symbolic action briefly takes on dramatic life, but the scenes of Talbot and his son generate their power as stylized renditions of an idea, as tableaux. Even the Temple Garden episode partakes more of this quality than of the character-centered drama that one associates with the later Shakespeare.

In its language the play illustrates the experimentation natural to a young writer. The styles include workaday verse, a pungently rough prose, a poetic aureation like Seneca and Ovid at their most extravagant, a more sedately lofty idiom, and even the amorous preciosity of Petrarchan verse. Although these styles have some function in the play, they are not used to create individual voices for the characters, except for Joan and perhaps a few others. The family remains an abstraction because the people who are involved in family relationships speak only in public tones. Its ideals are part of the value system of *1 Henry VI*, but its reality never takes on dramatic life. The road to *King Lear*, or to *1 Henry IV*, is a long one.

2 Henry VI

The surprising fact is how far along that road the second of the Henry VI plays progresses. In language and structure it is far more sophisticated than its predecessor, though at the cost of a certain untidiness. *2 Henry VI* is built on contrasts of character, especially between Henry and two other royal figures, Gloucester and York. These three divide the qualities of the ideal king—the virtues of the lion, the pelican, and the fox, as Tillyard calls them.[17] The contrast among the three is more elaborate than that between Talbot and Joan in *1 Henry VI*, and they are more fully and vividly developed than any characters in the earlier play. Once again Shakespeare illuminates the personal lives of these political figures through the family. The dramatic technique is much the same, though it displays greater skill and subtlety.

The language again includes diverse styles, but they

have a new dramatic function in establishing individual voices for the characters. The formal style of aureation and stock rhetoric dominates the hypocritical public speeches by Margaret and the plotting nobles, in contrast with their more direct and vehement private utterances. Or the same artificiality can express King Henry's ineffectual dallying with words at the cost of action. After helplessly watching the nobles arrest Gloucester for treason, he laments in the most precious of veins:

> Ay, Margaret; my heart is drown'd with grief,
> Whose flood begins to flow within mine eyes,
> My body round engirt with misery,
> For what's more miserable than discontent?
>
> (III.i.198-201)

In all the poetic idioms, references to the family support the dominant themes. The theme of disorder becomes more and more prominent not only in events but also in the poetry. References and images suggest that the civil strife infecting the commonwealth has spread through its whole body. The ordinary Englishman, who receives more attention in this play, suffers from the conflicts in the court. A group of petitioners to Gloucester have the misfortune to encounter Suffolk and the queen instead. Comic though it is, one man's complaint suggests how disorder is breeding injustice: "Mine is, an 't please your Grace, against John Goodman, my Lord Cardinal's man, for keeping my house, and lands, and wife, and all, from me" (I.iii.16-18). Suffolk and Margaret find the loss of his wife amusing and make no effort to help him.

When civil war finally breaks out with the Cade rebellion, such men are shown rising against established order. The consequences of their unnatural presumption appear in the proclamation for which Stafford calls:

> That those which fly before the battle ends
> May, even in their wives' and children's sight,
> Be hang'd up for example at their doors.
>
> (IV.ii.171-73)[18]

Earlier, in parting from Margaret, Suffolk recalls a different world, where children die peacefully in their mothers' arms:

> Here could I breathe my soul into the air,
> As mild and gentle as the cradle-babe
> Dying with mother's dug between his lips.
>
> (III.ii.390-92)

The artifice of his language helps to suggest the distance of this world, especially since it is the presumptuous adulterer Suffolk who thus recalls the sanctities of family living and dying.

Like the previous play, *2 Henry VI* emphasizes the theme of inheritance. When the Cardinal demands to be treated with respect as John of Gaunt's son, Gloucester bluntly reminds him of his bastardy (II.i.40-41). When Warwick accuses Suffolk of Gloucester's murder, the two exchange traditional insults about their mothers' chastity, with Suffolk outdoing the "Blunt-witted lord" in vigor and detail (III.ii.210-14, 221-22). This language of birth and inheritance has a parallel

in the characterization of Salisbury and his son Warwick, who illustrate the inheritance of virtue in a noble family. They confront the dilemma of all men of
good will in a disordered state, who can find no clear
object for their loyalty. They support Gloucester as
the main force for order and virtue, but when York
presents his claim to the throne, they feel obliged to
throw their backing to him. Warwick as yet shows
none of his kingmaker's arrogance, though there may
be some foreshadowing in his blunt pride. Now, however, he acts as the outspoken voice of simple hon-
esty, like Kent in *King Lear*.[19]

The first scene of the play establishes Salisbury as
a choric voice of English wisdom, and he is shown in
ideal harmony with his son: "Warwick, my son, the
comfort of my age" (I.i.189). When these men reveal
that they are supporting York's claim, it is a blow to
Henry, and he touches on moral inheritance in his
grieved outcry:

> Old Salisbury, shame to thy silver hair,
> Thou mad misleader of thy brain-sick son!
>
> (V.i.162-63)

Even that fundamental principle, the inheritance of
true nobility, seems to be corrupted in this anarchic
time. Whether or not Salisbury's choice for York is
correct (and the play does not decide that issue), he
is a man of good will. His son could become a mighty
force for good in an ordered community, another good
Duke Humphrey or Talbot, but in the weak reign of
Henry VI his immense energy turns into a disruptive

force. Warwick's degeneration from Salisbury's noble son to the arrogant, impulsive kingmaker suggests what is happening to the inherited virtue of England, the mighty tradition of Crécy and Agincourt to which these plays so often look back.

Thus the leitmotiv of inheritance is developed in characterization with Salisbury and Warwick. It is also used in the one obviously emblematic scene of this play, in which Alexander Iden kills Jack Cade. Cade's appearance marks the spread of anarchy to all of the commonwealth. Like Joan of Arc he shows the dregs of society making claim to lofty position in a prodigious manifestation of disorder. He too repudiates his actual parentage in order to claim high birth. (It is expressive of his popular roots that he concocts his story out of a folk motif, the fairy story of the abducted prince.) Also like Joan, he avows libertine naturalism, even substituting it officially for law: "There shall not a maid be married, but she shall pay to me her maidenhead, ere they have it. Men shall hold of me in capite; and we charge and command that their wives be as free as heart can wish or tongue can tell" (IV.vii.115-19). Cade is himself the threat that he predicts from the nobles when his followers are about to leave him: "Let them break your backs with burdens, take your houses over your heads, ravish your wives and daughters before your faces" (IV.viii.29-31).

When he staggers into Alexander Iden's garden, the types of order and disorder meet. In the symbolic garden that fascinates Shakespeare's imagination, Cade faces its owner, who has expressed his contentment with rural seclusion in a charming brief soliloquy:

THE HENRY VI PLAYS

Lord! who would live turmoiled in the court,
And may enjoy such quiet walks as these?
This small inheritance my father left me
Contenteth me, and worth a monarchy.

(IV.x.16-19)

Unlike Cade, Iden accepts his inheritance, about which he sounds a note common in Latin poetry, the quiet joy of country retreat. The victory of such a man over Jack Cade suggests that virtue is not lost to England, that it has merely fallen back to its rural fastnesses. Iden's quaintly artificial blank verse sets off Cade's vigorous prose, though the former never lives up to the pretty charm of the opening speech. In fact, Shakespeare seems to be so much fascinated with his tough-minded rebel that he gives him a wryly noble death, even at the expense of the emblematic picture. And at most this scene is a perfunctory expression of the ideal while civil strife dominates the dramatic foreground.[20]

Even more central than inheritance in *2 Henry VI* is marriage, which is of special importance for two of the chief kingly characters, Henry and Gloucester. In a way it is significant that York's wife does not appear; his detachment from the marital constraint that hampers his two rivals allows him to concentrate on single-minded pursuit of the crown. Only his sons keep York from being as solitary and unsocial a figure as Richard III, and at that he makes use of his sons' loyalty but shows little paternal affection. The grief for Rutland in *3 Henry VI*, stylized in expression as it is, makes the only exception to this coldness. One can hardly conceive of York with a wife, though of course she

57

does turn up in *Richard III*, when he is safely dead.

A passage in the first part of *An Homily Against Disobedience and Wilful Rebellion* illustrates both the Renaissance association between family and commonweal and the wife's divinely ordained role:

> Besides the obedience due unto his majesty, he not only ordained, that, in families and households, *the wife should be obedient unto her husband, the children unto their parents, the servants unto their masters;* but also, when mankind increased, and spread itself more largely over the world, he by his holy word did constitute and ordain in cities and countries several and special governors and rulers unto whom the residue of his people should be obedient.[21]

Both wives and governed are disobedient in this play. In a comic version of the theme Saunder Simpcox, the pretended blind man, is subservient to his officious wife, who keeps interrupting him to embellish his tale of how he was lamed. This comic episode is tied to the main plot by its occurrence just before the court learns of Eleanor's downfall.

Duke Humphrey is a powerful force for good, as the frequent punning references to his title of Protector suggest. His weakness is an innocence that leaves him vulnerable to the plots of other, more ambitious, people. When his wife warns him of the dangers around him, he assures her, "I must offend before I be attainted" (II.iv.59). Eleanor herself takes advantage of this weakness. Like the plotting nobles she is ambitious; she dresses more richly than the queen and even dreams of seizing the crown for her husband. Gloucester's rebuke to her arrogance is imperious; but when she starts to lose her temper, he quickly pacifies her, and she goes right on scheming. The conjuring scene (I.iv) exists largely to please the crowd with displays of magic and to foreshadow later deaths, but it also shows the Lord Protector's wife in the blasphemous act of calling up demons. When her enemies seize on her in this act and humiliate her, the shame of her penance subdues her pride, but by then it is too late to save Gloucester.

The disorder of the kingdom has tempted Eleanor to reach beyond her place in society. As a result, Gloucester is destroyed as a governor, and his marriage crumbles in his hands. His words weigh solemnly as he repudiates his union with treason:

> Noble she is, but if she have forgot
> Honour and virtue, and convers'd with such
> As, like to pitch, defile nobility,
> I banish her my bed and company,
> And give her as a prey to law and shame,
> That hath dishonour'd Gloucester's honest name.
>
> (II.i.186-91)

He has the simplicity of an older world, the days when a man needed only to be strong and loyal to his king. His wife adapts herself to the current morality of personal ambition, but she is not clever enough to survive against such adversaries as the Cardinal, Margaret, Suffolk, and York.

Shakespeare develops the relationship of Margaret and Henry at length over *2* and *3 Henry VI* after a

hasty beginning in the first play.[22] When Margaret
slaps her and provokes a quarrel, Eleanor pithily sums
up the queen's unnatural dominion over Henry:

> She'll hamper thee and dandle thee like a baby:
> Though in this place most master wear no breeches,
> She shall not strike Dame Eleanor unreveng'd.
>
> (I.iii.145-47)

In this untidy little courtly squabble Henry is, as usual,
ineffectually conciliatory. His weakness is apparent
when the two chief ladies of England vent their spite
by a quarrel in the king's presence.

2 Henry VI opens with a spectacular ceremony to
impress the importance of the marriage between
Henry and Margaret.[23] In every sense this is an unnatural union. Not only has the king neglected his
duty in wedding Margaret at all, but she will assume
an unwomanly dominon over him and form an adul-
terous liaison with Suffolk. When Henry receives her
from his "procurator," Suffolk, he echoes the amorous
preciosity of the end of *1 Henry VI* along with his
usual bland piety:

> I can express no kinder sign of love
> Than this kind kiss. O Lord, that lends me life,
> Lend me a heart replete with thankfulness!
> For thou hast given me in this beauteous face
> A world of earthly blessings to my soul,
> If sympathy of love unite our thoughts.
>
> (I.i.18-23)

The pun on "kinder" in the first line evokes the standard of nature by which this artificial ceremony is found wanting. Henry fuses Petrarchanism and piety in the tangled figure of a face that represents "earthly blessings" to a soul; the clumsiness of the poetry is in part justified by its suitability to Henry's confusion.

The first scene shows little of Margaret's character, since she makes only conventional speeches, but Gloucester's shock at the marriage contract makes clear the unsuitability of the terms. After the king and new queen go out in state, he delivers an impressive harangue in high oratorical style, one that rises through a series of rhetorical questions to a final impassioned exclamation:

> O peers of England! shameful is this league,
> Fatal this marriage, cancelling your fame,
> Blotting your names from books of memory,
> Razing the characters of your renown,
> Defacing monuments of conquer'd France,
> Undoing all, as all had never been!
>
> (97-102)

Henry's marriage has become a weapon destroying the traditional way of life, the noble code of chivalric glory. In a typically Shakespearian effect the Cardinal punctures Gloucester's loftiness with cynicism. But his opposition, which obviously springs from his animus toward Gloucester, cannot undermine the impression that the English peers overwhelmingly disapprove this match.

Having established the political inadequacy of the marriage, Shakespeare turns to Margaret's character in I.iii. She approaches in suspiciously close company

with Suffolk and then violates a right sacred to Englishmen by tearing up the petitions to the Lord Protector.[24] Like Queen Elinor in Peele's *Edward I,* she
is an arrogant foreign absolutist, as her question to
Suffolk establishes:

> My Lord of Suffolk, say, is this the guise,
> Is this the fashions in the court of England?
> (42-43)

Although she hates Gloucester and his wife as over-
weening subjects, she is not moved by any desire to
see Henry assume truly royal state. Suffolk promises
her that by the weeding of this garden of haughty
peers she herself will come to power. Thus the new
queen reveals herself, scornful of her husband's un-
manly piety and scheming with her paramour to take
control of the land.

Hereafter Margaret's voice largely merges with those
of the squabbling nobles. She is a skillful orator,
though sometimes her spite shows through too obviously to be missed even by Henry, who would be
glad not to perceive anything of ill feelings. She finds
Petrarchan idiom useful to manipulate his doting fondness for her. Thus she tries to distract him when it
seems that Suffolk may be in danger for Gloucester's
death. She embroiders with pretty sentimentality on
the stock theme of the lover's ship voyaging through
rough seas. One is willing to forgive Shakespeare the
slight inaccuracy when she associates herself with Dido
and Suffolk with Ascanius (rather than Cupid in disguise, as in Vergil; see III.ii.113-18). The ludicrous

audacity of turning the weakly pious Henry into the sternly "pius Aeneas" and her formidable self into poor "madding Dido" is too delicious to miss. After this speech it is hard to take seriously the rhetorical passion of her parting with Suffolk, but even this absurdity is later outdone when she draws on the apparently endless supply of bloody heads in Elizabethan theater to fondle that remnant of her dead lover in Henry's presence. The comic ineffectuality of his remonstrance is almost a justification for the episode:

> I fear me, love, if that I had been dead,
> Thou wouldest not have mourn'd so much for me.
> (IV.iv.22-23)

Her lover dead, Margaret begins to show an aggressive masculinity in her few remaining speeches, a development more completely shown in *3 Henry VI*. Even here she is a remarkable example of the forces that are undermining the state. She attacks all the values of the family—by her unfaithfulness to her husband; by her attempt to rule him and the land; and by her attack on the power and life of Gloucester, her husband's uncle and the last worthy representative of Henry V. Margaret of Anjou, the arrogant Frenchwoman, stands for everything that Henry V opposed. It is ominous for England that she and the Duke of York, the character whom she most resembles in temperament, dominate the two factions of Lancaster and York at the end of the play.

Conclusion.—2 Henry VI has a disorderly vitality

lacking in the First Part, and this vigor affects the handling of the family. One major concern is the theme of inheritance, which embraces the king himself, Salisbury and Warwick, Jack Cade, and Alexander Iden. Only the last remains a stylized, emblematic character. The relationship of Talbot and his son reappears in Salisbury and Warwick, but as these characters come to life, the thematic implications become richer and more complex. The earlier pair show the simple inheritance of virtue, untarnished by a corrupted state, but Salisbury and his son are more ambiguous. Warwick has more or less inherited his father's virtue, but the inheritance is corrupted by the political chaos that encourages his ambition. In different ways both Henry and Jack Cade show this same distortion of inheritance and natural succession.

Of the two important marriages in the play, Shakespeare gives the greater complexity and depth to that of Henry and Margaret; but its implications extend into *3 Henry VI*, whereas the study of Gloucester and Eleanor is largely within this play. Gloucester can no more control his wife's ambition than he can maintain order and degree in the commonwealth. Her usurpation of manly concerns shows in little what is happening in the kingdom. She and the other ambitious and mannish women of these plays show that in a collapsing social order women cannot fulfill their natural and traditional functions. In Henry's court, love is either a deceit or a weakness. Margaret's love language can have no meaning except as a mask. The strongest man in the play, Richard, Duke of York, is the one least encumbered with traditional emotions and loyalties. Although these characters are more vital than those in *1 Henry VI* (even the same people), none of them is so strong as the impersonal force that dominates events, the historical power that drives England nearer and nearer to chaos. In this least Senecan play of the first tetralogy, what is most like Seneca is this sense of a fatal curse dominating men's actions. Past events and dead men lurk in the background, and in the last two plays their presence will be felt even more.

3 Henry VI

The disorder reaches its climax in the last of the Henry VI plays, which has neither the mechanical structure of the first part nor the balanced characters of the second. Insofar as it achieves a unified effect, it does so by its theme and, ultimately, by its poetic language. Not figures but acts and events are balanced against each other. The characters lose themselves in the welter of words and action—all but one, that is. For Richard, Duke of Gloucester, stands out from the fabric of the play in a way that imperils its dramatic and poetic proportion even while creating a high point of dramatic interest. Nevertheless, what is most impressive about the play is not the emerging Richard, who has freer rein in the next, but its attainment of poetic unity without entirely sacrificing the remarkable diversity of poetic modes in *2 Henry VI*.

The family is more prominent as emblem and symbol in this part than in the previous two. It is so richly woven through the language that it helps greatly in the unity of effect that this play achieves. One objective measure of its importance is the frequent occurrence of eight common nouns of family relationship—brother, daughter, father, husband, mother, sister, son, and wife. They appear 228 times in *3 Henry VI*, nearly three times as often as in each of the other two Henry VI plays. Only *Richard III*, a play similar in technique, compares in frequency among all the histories with its 256 occurrences. Of course, statistics like these are only a crude measure of the importance of the family, but such wide variations surely indicate a remarkable concentration of references in the last two plays of the tetralogy.

The specific content of references to the family varies greatly. Clifford draws on the doctrine of correspondences to prove from animal behavior how immoral is Henry's willingness to disinherit his son. After citing the lion, the bear, the serpent, the worm, the dove, and even their enemy York as good parents, he makes the application specific: "For shame, my liege, make them your precedent!" (II.ii.33). Richard, Duke of Gloucester, draws on his stock of proverbs to chide his brother Edward's foolish marriage: "Yet hasty marriage seldom proveth well" (IV.i.18). Clarence uses biblical lore, the tale of Jephthah, to justify breaking his oath to his father-in-law and thus evokes the terrible image of a father sacrificing his daughter (V.i.93-94). Clifford in his dying speech cites the myth of Phaëthon as a classical parallel to Henry's failure as son and heir of Henry V (II.vi.11-13).[25] More ingeniously handled is a reference to Daedalus and

Icarus in the scene of Henry's death. Richard introduces the story with characteristic bluntness and punning.

> Why, what a peevish fool was that of Crete,
> That taught his son the office of a fowl!
> And yet, for all his wings, the fool was drown'd.
>
> (V.vi.18-20)

Henry picks up the thread with his usual poetic prettiness and turns the allusion into a schematic allegory (21-25). Here at least Shakespeare adjusts the classical decoration to the distinctive voices of the two characters. As these different uses illustrate, the family theme pervades all the poetic modes of the play.

Underlying this pattern in the language is constant emphasis on a few key ideas, the themes of disorder and corrupted marriage and inheritance. Thus frequent references to disorder in the family suggest the chaos to which civil war has brought England.[26] Since the poles of this disorder are two men, Henry in his weakness and Richard in his evil strength, a reference to the effect of each of them on the family will illustrate the technique. The dying Clifford asserts that if Henry had not been a weak king,

> I, and ten thousand in this luckless realm
> Had left no mourning widows for our death.
>
> (II.vi.18-19)

And when Henry is about to die, he prophesies of Richard:

And many an old man's sigh, and many a widow's,
And many an orphan's water-standing eye—
Men for their sons', wives for their husbands',
Orphans for their parents' timeless death—
Shall rue the hour that ever thou wast born.

(V.vi.39-43)

Both speeches emphasize the sheer number of those who are to suffer rather than the intensity of the individuals' grief. The abstractness of the images is in keeping with the lofty Senecan mode. Most of the references to the family are of this sort, though the most striking examples gain force from their dramatic context. The themes of marriage and inheritance are also present in this play, but they are more thoroughly woven into complexes of character and action. The language is less a separable element than in *2 Henry VI*, even while it plays a bigger role.

The last of the Henry VI plays has the most impressive of the emblematic scenes, one that helps to enrich the many references to the family. At the battlefield of Towton, Henry soliloquizes on the woes that he has brought to himself and England. Then he overhears and joins in the laments of a father who has killed his son and a son who has killed his father. Unlike the emblematic scenes with Talbot and Alexander Iden, this episode comes early in the action (II.v). Partly as a consequence, the play afterward loses emotional momentum until it picks up toward the end. Henry's soliloquy itself is charming to modern taste; but Sir Barry Jackson, commenting on his production of *2* and *3 Henry VI* in Birmingham, defends their decision to include the scene of the fathers and sons as well: "The poet's infallible intuition, however, proved right. The scene was retained, but treated as a static tableau: it shone away and above the violent episodes with which it is surrounded and threw more light on the horror of civil war than all the scenes of wasteful bloodshed."[27] *3 Henry VI* is the most iterative of Shakespeare's history plays, with its insistence on the theme of disorder. Hence the suddenly expansive effect of this scene, with its different mode of expressing the theme, is all the more striking.

After the scurrying to and fro of Scenes iii and iv, the sudden shift to Henry's soliloquy is like an orator's dramatic lowering of his voice. Clifford's challenge to Richard has just shown the usual idiom of the play:

> This is the hand that stabb'd thy father York,
> And this the hand that slew thy brother Rutland;
> And here's the heart that triumphs in their death
> And cheers these hands, that slew thy sire and brother,
> To execute the like upon thyself.
>
> (II.iv.6-10)

In the elaborate nature simile with which Henry begins, Shakespeare not only gives all this violence a sudden distance, but suggests the realm of the pastoral, to which Henry will explicitly turn. His solitary position on a molehill is appropriate to this weak man who is the center of the struggle, yet who has been chidden from the field because he does his cause more harm than good.

His words give an idyllic view of the shepherd's

orderly life and the natural fecundity with which it is associated. The shepherd is of course a traditional symbol for benign leadership, whether Christ or the governor; thus in *2 Henry VI* Humphrey, Duke of Gloucester, is "the shepherd of the flock" (II.ii.72). But Henry's wish for the pastoral life is ironic, since it undermines what the symbol in this sense represents, the guiding role of the king. He is disrupting the order of the state in seeking the orderly life of tending flocks. At the same time Shakespeare is careful to give the wish poignance; as always, he shows a deep understanding of the king's inevitable loneliness. For this purpose he uses the pastoral theme in a way characteristic of Seneca and countless others, contrasting the safety of humble life with the peril of lofty position.

The soliloquy also provides a fine tonal modulation. Its artificiality is to some extent psychological, a manifestation of Henry's escapism, but it prepares the way for the full-blown ritualism of the episode with the fathers and sons. With this shift to a more abstract dramatic level, Shakespeare gives one of the recurrent images of the play pictorial form. The many images of disorder in the family come together in a symbolic action that vivifies them all. At the same time, the scene directs attention to the thematic significance of the family relationships of the main characters, especially the fathers and sons—Henry and Prince Edward, the two Cliffords, and York and his sons. Much more than the Talbot-and-son episode of *1 Henry VI*, this scene expresses in emblematic form the theme of the play.

Even within the passage one can see the movement

from the specific to the idealized and general. The first speeches of the son and father are more detailed and less stylized than Henry's formal lamentations at the end of each. Also the son's speech is more exact in biographical detail than the father's. The latter moves from bemoaning his son to a wider vision:

> O pity, God, this miserable age!
> What stratagems, how fell, how butcherly,
> Erroneous, mutinous, and unnatural,
> This deadly quarrel daily doth beget!
>
> (88-91)

The language may at first seem simple, yet it has considerable rhetorical pattern. What is first noticeable is the series of adjectives building up to the key word "unnatural." The aural play of "deadly" and "daily" in the last line suggests with the word "beget" that natural forces have been perverted, turned to breeding chaos. The passage demonstrates Shakespeare's skill at interweaving Latinate and English terms, not only in the series of adjectives but also in the pairing of "pity" and "miserable," which suggests its Latin sense. This last device evokes the language of liturgy, a kind of stylization toward which the whole passage moves.

Henry's choral response to this lamentation is longer, more general, and more artificial than that to the son's. He begins on the note with which he ended before, closing the line with the same word, "grief," and then goes on to amplify a familiar emblem:

> Woe above woe! grief more than common grief!
> O that my death would stay these ruthful deeds!

O pity, pity, gentle heaven, pity!
The red rose and the white are on his face,
The fatal colours of our striving houses:
The one his purple blood right well resembles;
The other his pale cheeks, methinks, presenteth.
Wither one rose, and let the other flourish!
If you contend, a thousand lives must wither.

(94-102)

Here the king's conventional prettiness of idiom suggests the tone of the previous soliloquy, but the artificiality is less ironic because of the generally formal
context and the contact with the theme of the play.
No longer out of touch with the reality around him,
Henry is expressing the disorder of civil war. This is
the paradox of his nature, that despite his failure as a
king his personal goodness and piety enable him to
see better than those around him the nature of the
forces sweeping through England. Especially striking
is the image that makes the dynastic quarrel of York
and Lancaster parasitic on the life of the nation. After
a conventional poetic game with the red and white
roses evokes the submerged metaphor of the state as a
garden, the last line makes the growth of the two rival
plants destructive of the whole garden.

What follows is hard for us to understand and harder
yet to manage on the modern stage: the king, father,
and son chant an antiphonal chorus of lamentation.
The technique has its roots in the morality play and
Seneca's scenes of lamentation, but Shakespeare's combination of severe regularity with simplicity of means
is not really comparable with either. Again one is
most directly reminded of liturgy and the *Book of*

Common Prayer. The Talbot-and-son scenes are much more "literary." The rhymed stichomythy there, as is almost inevitable, gives a sense of premeditation and artfulness. The attitudes of the father and son are too obviously the stock responses of heroes in books. It is indicative of the muted poetic means in the later scene that Shakespeare avoids couplets except to cap the episode. The two ostentatious classicisms, the Latinate pun on "obsequious" in line 118 and the allusion to Priam's grief for his sons in line 120, are obtrusive. One should not so much listen to the speakers' words as respond to the symbolic picture of King Henry sitting on his molehill and the father and son kneeling beside their victims, all mourning. The father and son are nameless because they are England. Even Henry for once transcends his weakness and in his grief becomes the king and father of a suffering land. Thus for a moment the play shifts to a level of powerful abstraction.

It is with grim irony that the action resumes and the normal view of Henry returns. The first speaker after this antiphony is Prince Edward, the son whom Henry has disinherited and whom his weakness will shortly destroy. The king relapses into his normal, blandly conciliating manner and hurries off after being bullied by Margaret and Exeter. In the normal life of this play the only kind of antiphony is parodic, as in the next scene, when the victors mockingly lament over Clifford's body. Their sarcastic echoing of the themes of mercy and father-and-son emphasizes that they are immersed in the violent strife, that ceremony and ritual have no meaning for them:

Rich. Clifford, ask mercy, and obtain no grace.
Edw. Clifford, repent in bootless penitence.
War. Clifford, devise excuses for thy faults.
Geo. While we devise fell tortures for thy faults.
Rich. Thou didst love York, and I am son to York.
Edw. Thou pitied'st Rutland, I will pity thee.

(II.vi.69-74)

Here as elsewhere the perversion of ceremony is a sign of the corruption of all meaningful order. In a play marked by these parodic ceremonies, only the visionary Henry can detach himself from the violence to partake of a genuine ritual, one that evokes the standards of order by which these bloody rivals are finally judged.

The themes of marriage and inheritance are both important in *3 Henry VI*. As visionary, Henry may rise above the others; but as husband and father, he epitomizes the disorder of the commonwealth. His wife's infidelity with Suffolk is not forgotten, for Edward calls her a Helen to Henry's Menelaus (II.ii.146-49), and York compares her to "an Amazonian trull" (I.iv.114). This last insult also suggests what is more prominent in this play, her unnatural assumption of a masculine role, in effect usurping her husband's kingship. It is she who gathers an army to oppose York's enforced settlement after the battle of Saint Albans. She will not allow her husband to speak before the battle of Towton, or to be present at the battle, lest he demoralize the army. But even this inverted marriage is shaken by Henry's weakness. Since *2 Henry VI* began with the formal ceremony of their marriage, the effect is all the more powerful when in the first scene of this play she formally renounces her husband because he has disinherited his son. It is ironic that Margaret should thus appeal to the sanctions of the family. They have a purely verbal currency among these selfish and ambitious conspirators, who flagrantly ignore them in practice. In defeat Margaret will earn our sympathy, yet there is a fierce justice in her being forced to see her son stabbed to death.

In a schematic parallel with Henry's rash marriage, Edward is moved by lust to neglect a prudent match for a foolish one. The lust of this "bluntest wooer in Christendom" (III.ii.83) lacks even the disguise of Petrarchan language. He is unscrupulous enough to use Lady Grey's affection for her children in his attempt to seduce her. The bawdy humor in this episode undermines in advance Warwick's formal proposal of affiance to the Lady Bona, and the ceremonial wedding procession at IV.i. seems especially hollow. Warwick's speech to King Lewis reflects the Petrarchan idiom:

> Myself have often heard him say, and swear,
> That this his love was an eternal plant,
> Whereof the root was fix'd in Virtue's ground,
> The leaves and fruit maintain'd with Beauty's sun.
> (III.iii.123-26)

But such poetic embellishments are more and more separate from the reality of behavior and motive. This language is not merely a poetic smokescreen for a state marriage that will later be broken off, as in *1 Henry VI*. Here the "eternal plant" has already found new ground in which to root. Again the only valid ceremonial language is the mock ceremony of Lewis's and the Lady Bona's replies to Edward.

Like his rival, Edward proves his weakness as a king by a foolish marriage; and Warwick, now an enemy, spells out the political consequences:

> Alas! how should you govern any kingdom
> That know not how to use ambassadors,
> Nor how to be contented with one wife,
> Nor how to use your brothers brotherly?
>
> (IV.iii.35-38)

The last line refers to the damage that Edward's uxoriousness inflicts on his brothers. As Clarence says, "But in your bride you bury brotherhood" (IV.i.54). The consequence is that Edward loses Clarence's support, and Richard stays with him only to usurp the crown. If this brother destroys Edward's hope for a peaceful succession, the retribution is appropriate to his misdeeds, a pattern reiterated to the point of tediousness in this play and *Richard III*.

The most important family theme in this play is inheritance, of which Clifford gives the orthodox doctrine: "Who should succeed the father but the son?" (II.ii.94). The words "father" and "son" occur 137 times, the references centering on the two rival houses. In the first scene their rights of inheritance are disputed at length. Henry's descent from the warrior king Henry V is his main claim to the throne. Even York's supporter Warwick does not attack the dead hero, but he is quick to point out that Henry VI is not his father's moral inheritor. Henry V's virtue has been lost to his country; the suggestion may be that Henry VI's weakness is a delayed effect of the curse on his grandfather's usurpation. Exeter's decision to support York's title emphasizes that the right of inheritance cannot be bartered away by men. In the curiously repetitive structure of *3 Henry VI,* the gist of this discussion is repeated when Warwick debates Margaret and her followers at the French court, where Oxford traces Henry's heroic lineage back to a John of Gaunt unhistorically given Spanish conquests.[28]

Nothing was more sacred in Elizabethan eyes and more firmly established by law than the son's right of inheritance. One of Henry's weakest acts is to disinherit his son in favor of York. Both he and Margaret refer to his deed as unnatural in the first scene, and she renounces their marriage on that ground. Prince Edward completes the destruction of natural order when he too repudiates his father to follow his mother into battle. Curiously enough, however, the young prince more than his father is Henry V's moral heir. At the battle of Tewkesbury his courageous words inspire Oxford to exclaim:

> O brave young Prince! thy famous grandfather
> Doth live again in thee: long may'st thou live
> To bear his image and renew his glories!
>
> (V.iv.52-54)

He gives a very different view of moral inheritance from Henry's defense of abandoning his son's claim to the throne:

> And happy always was it for that son

Whose father for his hoarding went to hell?
I'll leave my son my virtuous deeds behind;
And would my father had left me no more!

(II.ii.47-50)

These words might seem to express the highest piety
and wisdom. After all, Henry cannot deny that his
title to the throne is weak. Yet his father has left him
not just the English crown but a tradition of glorious
rule and conquest. He is losing the moral heritage of
Agincourt just as surely as his reign has lost the terri-
torial gains. The knighting of Prince Edward is necessarily a flawed ceremony, since he cannot fight only
for the right if he is to defend the greatness of his own
heritage. He is trapped by his great-grandfather's
usurpation, and the tainting of his moral inheritance
is completed by Margaret's questionable ancestry.

In an ordered society the son can by emulation learn
his forebears' virtue even while he takes over their
social position. But in the chaos of *3 Henry VI* moral
order is dissolved; the forces of inheritance are perverted to an unnatural function, the perpetuation of
a curse. Not only does this distortion affect the two
rival houses, but it encompasses the supporting nobles
of each side. One recurrent event includes a son who
commits violence in revenge for the death of his father
or some other member of his family.[29] Both times that
Henry's title to the crown is discussed at length, a
noble vows to support him whether or not it is weak,
because the Yorkists have killed the noble's father.
Oxford, who thus answers Warwick at III.iii.101-5, is
left relatively untainted by this motive; but Clifford

(I.i.165-66) is led to commit the most brutal act of a violent play. When he encounters the youngest son of his enemy York, he declares:

> As for the brat of this accursed duke,
> Whose father slew my father, he shall die.
>
> (I.iii.4-5)

This theme becomes obsessive in the many debates between such opponents as Clifford and York's sons about who is fighting whom in revenge for what butchered relatives.

Much subtler is the treatment of the House of York, to which the center of attention shifts as the Lancastrian power fades. Early in the play the loyalty of York's sons seems a remarkable exception to the destruction of traditional bonds. Edward and Richard show apparently sincere concern about their father's welfare, the latter revealing even a kind of hero-worship: "Methinks 'tis prize enough to be his son" (II.i.20). The omen of three suns merging into one gives cosmic endorsement to the unity of York's three heirs. Is it possible that this family, rightful heirs to the throne, are not infected by the general disorder? They seem to uphold the ideal expressed by Stefano Guazzo: "There is nothing which so much maintaineth the honour of houses, as the agreement amongst brothers."[30] Their success applies the critical test, for all three brothers begin to pursue their individual ends when Edward reaches the throne.

Shakespeare gives perfunctory attention to Clarence's wavering. Because of ambition and anger at slights by Edward, Clarence entangles himself in a new family loyalty by marrying Warwick's daughter. His dilemma of loyalties is summed up by the repetition of "father" in his ceremonial repudiation of Warwick's cause:

George takes the red rose from his hat and throws it at Warwick.

> Father of Warwick, know you what this means?
> Look, here I throw my infamy at thee;
> I will not ruinate my father's house,
> Who gave his blood to lime the stones together,
> And set up Lancaster.
>
> (V.i.84-88)

The irony is all the richer if one follows Andrew Cairncross and Peter Alexander in using the quarto staging of the incident. After Clarence declares for Warwick, Richard in pantomime seduces him into changing sides.[31] Whether or not his reform of conscience is purely hypocritical, there is a powerful irony in the greeting of Richard, who by now has established his villainy: "Welcome, good Clarence; this is brother-like" (108). Opposite this brotherly corruption in the Yorks is the truly fraternal attachment expressed by the dying words of Warwick and Montague in the next scene.

Richard, Duke of Gloucester, is the final inheritor of the York cause, and his attitude toward the family most fully expresses the corruption of his house. He reveals himself at length in *Richard III*, but *3 Henry VI* raises an interesting technical question: how can the loyal son of the early acts be reconciled with the ruthless schemer who emerges in the soliloquy of III.ii? Even Margaret implies his devotion to his father when she taunts the latter with his helplessness:

> And where's that valiant crook-back prodigy,
> Dicky your boy, that with his grumbling voice
> Was wont to cheer his dad in mutinies?
>
> (I.iv.75-77)

But this speech also hints at the other side of Richard's character, that he is a "prodigy," a perversion of nature. Neither he nor anyone else can forget his distorted body and the unnatural portents of his birth. Margaret baits him:

> But thou art neither like thy sire nor dam,
> But like a foul misshapen stigmatic.
>
> (II.ii.135-36)

Richard gives memorable expression to the same idea in the soliloquy that establishes his demonic force:

> Why, Love forswore me in my mother's womb:
> And, for I should not deal in her soft laws,
> She did corrupt frail Nature with some bribe,
>
> .   .   .   .
>
> To disproportion me in every part,
> Like to a chaos, or unlick'd bear-whelp
> That carries no impression like the dam.
>
> (III.ii.153-62)

He is specifically talking of sexual love, but his unnatural birth and monstrous growth alienate him from all affection. His final soliloquy powerfully sums up his isolation from everything human:

> Then, since the heavens have shap'd my body so,
> Let hell make crook'd my mind to answer it.
> I have no brother, I am like no brother;
> And this word 'love,' which greybeards call divine,
> Be resident in men like one another,
> And not in me: I am myself alone.
>
> (V.vi.78-83)

His words repudiate the last vestiges of order and morality. He embodies the evil toward which the others have been drifting. Because they hold on to some few shreds of affection and humanity, he dismisses them as sentimentalists. Entirely single-minded in his ambition, he is the most powerful force left in England: "I am myself alone." In one sense he is a monster created by heaven to punish the land, but in another he is the natural product of the whole descent toward chaos.

Still, the problem of Richard's change of character is unanswered. The simplest explanation is that in the puzzling early speeches he is merely a type, an expression of the family loyalty of the Yorks, whereas later he becomes an independent character. In most of his speeches he has a distinctive poetic idiom, but his expressions of concern for his father are conventional and artificially elevated. This early nature could reflect what Samuel Bethell calls depersonalization;[32] Richard loses his identity in order to express a general theme. The family loyalty of the Yorks must be established at first so that its collapse may illustrate the consequences of rebellion. One question about this explanation is why Shakespeare uses the most individual of the three sons to express loyalty to York. Clarence, for example, is a shadowy enough figure that he could have voiced Richard's sentiments in II.i without appearing notably inconsistent, yet he is not even present.

On the other hand, there is a more elaborately psychological explanation. From his first appearance in *2 Henry VI* Richard is a powerful force, one who slices through the cant of those around him in a single-minded pursuit of whatever seems important to him. As the early Warwick illustrates, such a man can be a strong support for order and virtue if something larger than himself attracts his loyalty. York is the only man in *3 Henry VI* whose ambition and strength of will are enough to compel Richard's support. Although his son can teach York something of Machiavellian casuistry (I.ii.22-34), York's massive violence of nature is worthy of Richard's respect. It is the most powerful force of the early civil wars. Richard never expresses without irony an attachment to anyone but his father. When the strength of his nature is freed from its filial tie, the last remnant of an order into which he can fit, he inevitably becomes a destructive force.

This argument is translatable into political terms. Whether or not York has a good title to the throne, he is a rebel, and rebellion breeds more of itself. As Dostoyevsky shows in *The Devils*, the second generation of revolutionaries is more demonic than the first. Richard is exactly right when he avows, "I am son to York" (II.vi.73), but his inheritance is perverted. The disorder that his father must foment he carries to new lengths, not only in the state but also in the family. One curious fact about him is that he is most human—and most like his father—in the heat of battle. It is in the conspiracies of the court that he goes beyond any evil yet shown in these plays. Thus there is a psychological and political validity in Richard's change, though it seems inadequate to explain the fullness of his malevolence. There is also a thematic justification for the change in order to express a paradox in the origin of evil. Human categories of causation cannot explain the full power of evil. Rebellion breeds disorder by a natural process, but sometimes it releases a demonic power whose generation is finally mysterious.

All these explanations have some truth, yet they are not totally satisfying. Shakespeare may well have had these ideas about Richard or something like them, but he has not really embodied them in dramatic action. We do not see Richard becoming a monster; we only see him as son and then as monster. Change in the state and change between generations are important themes in *3 Henry VI*, but change in character has not yet enlisted Shakespeare's full imaginative powers.[33] This is not finally a play of character but of atmosphere, the atmosphere of disorder and chaos.

The corruption of the House of York is apparent in one final irony, the false dawn with which the play ends. When the Yorkists murder Prince Edward before his mother's eyes, she cries out a curse on their children. Only a score of lines later Edward says of his queen, "By this, I hope, she hath a son for me" (V.v.88). With pomp and circumstance the last scene of the play reveals the king, the queen, and this new heir to the throne. Edward proclaims the triumph of the York cause in the last lines of the play:

> Sound drums and trumpets! Farewell, sour annoy!
> For here, I hope, begins our lasting joy.
>
> (V.vii.45-46)

But the image that remains is of the crook-backed Richard kissing his nephew. Order in the family and the state may seem to have been restored, but the appearance is illusory. The chain of guilt is too strong to be broken without still more violence and suffering for England.

Conclusion.—Far from being an incoherent piece of chronicling, *3 Henry VI* is an ordered drama, though it is not, like *2 Henry VI,* built on the usual Shakespearian method of character development and contrast. The theme of political disorder informs the entire structure, and the primary symbol is disorder in the family. If anything, the iterative technique of the play is monotonous with its countless allusions to the destruction of family bonds, the meaninglessness of marriage, and the corruption of inheritance in a realm where there is no strong king who commands unquestioned loyalty. The poetic variety of the previous play is here subdued to this overriding tone, though Richard has a poetic idiom more distinctive than any in

2 Henry VI. Except for him there is a loss in vitality, but that is compensated for by a gain in brooding power. The monolithic integrity of the work is reminiscent of Seneca's plays at their best. Also Shakespeare is developing the technique of irony, which later becomes immensely rich. As yet it is often rather crude, but even now it is valuable as an organizing principle. Perhaps because Richard III is superlatively built on a similar pattern, the structural skill of 3 Henry VI has been too little appreciated.

[1] Shakespeare, Politics and Politicians, English Association Pamphlet No. 72 (Oxford, Eng., 1929), p. 8.

[2] Shakespeare's History Plays (London, 1944), esp. pp. 147-61.

[3] G. Wilson Knight, The Olive and the Sword (New York, 1944), p. 10.

[4] Cf. Hugh Dickinson, "Shakespeare's Henry-Yea-and-Nay," Drama Critique 4 (1961), 68-72.

[5] Construction in Shakespeare (Ann Arbor, Mich., 1951), p. 26.

[6] The Jacobean Shakespeare and Measure for Measure, Annual Shakespeare Lecture of the British Academy (London, 1937), p. 8.

[7] Both the Cairncross and Wilson (New Cambridge) editions read "Falstaff" as in the Folio, though most editors emend to "Fastolfe" as in the chronicles.

[8] See The First Part of King Henry VI, New Arden Edition (Cambridge, Mass., 1962), note at II.iii.22.

[9] Sigurd Burckhardt has some stimulating remarks on the significance of this scene for our perception of Talbot, though I think he exaggerates its uniqueness in the play and his theological conclusions seem farfetched. See "'I Am But Shadow of Myself': Ceremony and Design in 1 Henry VI," Shakespearean Meanings (Princeton, N.J., 1968), pp. 47-77. David M. Bevington is thoughtful and moderate in "The Domineering Female in 1 Henry VI," Shakespeare Studies 2 (1966), 51-58.

[10] Shakespeare omits the fact, reported in Hall, that Talbot had a

bastard son, Henry Talbot, killed in the same battle. Edward Hall, *Hall's Chronicle* (London, 1809), p. 229.

[11] Tillyard, p. 172.

[12] *The Complete Works of George Gascoigne*, ed. John W. Cunliffe (Cambridge, Eng., 1907), I, 291.

[13] *The First Part of King Henry VI*, New Cambridge Shakespeare (Cambridge, Eng., 1952), pp. xlv-xlvii.

[14] Cf. Cairncross's note on the passage.

[15] See, for example, "The Booke of Matrimony," *The Worckes of Thomas Becon* (London, 1564), I, 618 ff. Henry's violation of the earlier spousals makes this marriage even more suspect.

[16] Cairncross, *1 Henry VI*, p. xliv.

[17] Tillyard, pp. 185-86.

[18] The idea that rebels meet such a fate is a truism, often found in the *Homilies*, for example: "For first, the rebels do not only dishonour their prince, the parent of their country, but also do dishonour and shame their natural parents, if they have any, do shame their kindred and friends, do disherit and undo for ever their children and heirs" ("The Third Part of the Homily Against Disobedience and Wilful Rebellion," *Certain Sermons or Homilies Appointed to Be Read in Churches* [Oxford, Eng., 1822], p. 525).

[19] Tillyard, pp. 182-83, creates an unnecessary difficulty by assuming that Salisbury and Warwick know of the plot to murder Gloucester. Surely they are not intended to stand silently by during the planning at III.i.223 ff. (The quarto has them exit with the king.) From York at II.ii.72-74 they learn only what everyone knows, that most of the court is scheming toward Gloucester's overthrow; nothing is said of his murder. Hence Warwick's indignation on finding his body is neither feigned nor out of character.

[20] Cf. J. P. Brockbank, "The Frame of Disorder: *Henry VI*," *Early Shakespeare*, ed. John Russell Brown and Bernard Harris, Stratford-Upon-Avon Studies No. 3 (London, 1961), pp. 89-90.

[21] *Homilies*, p. 508.

[22] There is just a hint of Gloucester's uxoriousness as well. At I.i.39-40 the Cardinal sneers: "Thy wife is proud; she holdeth thee in awe / More than God or religious churchmen may."

[23] As Brockbank points out, Holinshed traces the beginning of Henry VI's woes to this marriage (*Early Shakespeare*, p. 82). Hall has a similar sentiment; see *Hall's Chronicle*, p. 204.

[24] Or at least she is a party to the action if the quarto verson is correct. See Cairncross's note at I.iii.39.

[25] Erasmus illustrates the allegorical reading of this myth when he interprets Phaëthon as "a prince, who while still headstrong with the ardor of youth, but with no supporting wisdom, seized the reins of government and turned everything into ruin for himself and the whole world" (*The Education of a Christian Prince*, trans. Lester K. Born [New York, 1936], p. 147). This allegorical tradition may help to explain why the same myth is, as H. C. Hart's note at I.iv.33 remarks, "unmercifully lugged in" by Clifford to describe York's downfall (*The Third Part of King Henry the Sixth*, Arden Shakespeare [London, 1910]).

[26] Cf. Cairncross, *The Third Part of King Henry VI*, New Arden Edition (Cambridge, Mass., 1964), p. liii.

[27] "On Producing *Henry VI*," *Shakespeare Survey*, 6 (1953), p. 51.

[28] The same legend occurs in the *Spanish Tragedy*. The two references may reflect a popular tradition, as Hart suggests in his note at III.iii.81-82.

[29] Ronald S. Berman writes (specifically of *2 Henry VI*): "In order to demonstrate devotion and filial piety man must change the moral standards of loyalty to those of the vendetta" ("Fathers and Sons in the Henry VI Plays," *Shakespeare Quarterly* 13 [1962], 490).

[30] *The Civile Conversation of M. Steeven Guazzo*, trans. George Pettie and Bartholomew Young, Vol. VIII, The Tudor Translations, 2d ser. (New York, 1925), II, 89.

[31] For Alexander's version see *William Shakespeare: The Complete Works*, The Tudor Shakespeare (London, 1951).

[32] *Shakespeare and the Popular Dramatic Tradition* (New York, 1944), pp. 90 ff.

[33] Cf. Robert Y. Turner, "Characterization in Shakespeare's Early History Plays," *ELH* 31 (1964), 241-58.

Chapter III

RICHARD III

I N *Richard III,* the climax of the first historical tetralogy, Shakespeare weaves the strands of the earlier plays into a full artistic unity. Whatever the merits of the Henry VI plays, they are seldom performed; and whatever the limitations of *Richard III* compared to the later masterpieces, it is one of the most popular plays in the canon. Sir Thomas More's fine ironic portrait of an evil king gave Shakespeare rich material to work from. Having a dominant protagonist implicit in the source may have freed him from some of the perils of the chronicle form. He may have learned from Marlowe how to shape a play around a great villain. But however the growth came about, the poetic and dramatic patterns of the tetralogy here attain a new concentration. The family, as important a presence in this play as in *3 Henry VI,* contributes to the new unity of effect.

What gives order to *Richard III* is the central conflict between the villain-king and the power of nemesis. This vengeful force has some effect on the consciousness of Richard himself; but it is primarily an external force, embodied in the curses, the wailing women, and the figure of Richmond as God's minister. Although the concept of nemesis is in part Senecan, Shakespeare fuses this classical power with Christian Providence. Thus he tempers the melodrama of Thyestes' creator with the sober moralism of Edward Hall and the authors of *A Mirror for Magistrates*.[1] One might see Margaret as a more realistic version of the Senecan ghost, but as the play goes on, Richmond and the Yorkist women take over her role as the spokesmen of nemesis.

Also Richard himself is by no means an ordinary Senecan villain swept by passion. In the first place, he has the qualities of the Elizabethan Machiavel, a modification of Seneca's rulers to emphasize their disruptive effect on the orthodox political order. What takes him out of the ranks of Elizabethan Senecanism, however, is his connection with the traditional Vice, the stock villain of the morality plays.[2] Whereas the Senecan tyrant rages against virtue in the name of ambition or lust, Richard, "like the formal vice, Iniquity" (III.i.82), thrives by an ironic detachment from all the standards of traditional morality, including the claims of the family. Like Politic Persuasion in John Phillip's *Patient Grissell*, he undermines the bonds of natural love by his plots. Richard shares with the Vice his consummate hypocrisy and his demonic sense of humor, both of which exploit the morality of the family. Thus he draws on three traditions of evil: the Senecan villain for his personal forcefulness and powerful position, the Machiavellian schemer for his political nihilism, and the morality Vice for his ironic detachment from human feeling. Shakespeare's villain

is a formidable opponent for the nemesis of the play,
not just a tool of superhuman forces.

The main role of the family in *Richard III* is to
make nemesis more than just a Senecan doom, to give
it weight and ethical meaning as a force of Providence.
Richard's demonism shows itself in his attacks on the
family; and a marriage, the union of Richmond and
Queen Elizabeth's daughter, symbolizes the triumph
of Providence. Even before this union the opposition
to Richard speaks through the wailing women, who
call on the moral standards of the family. Their scenes
of lamentation use the ritualistic technique of the
Henry VI plays with its appeal to traditional morality
and religion, but the ritualistic scenes in *Richard III*
have an even more central place in developing the
theme. The scenes of lamentation and the character of
Richard are the two poles around which the language
of the play clusters, though references to the family
pervade the entire play.

If *Richard III* achieves a uniquely English and popular Senecanism, one of the main reasons is its language. The clumsy and merely decorative classical allusions of the Henry VI plays have largely vanished,[3]
and the tricks of formal rhetoric are adapted to a
thoroughly English idiom. What *The Spanish Tragedy*
does for the Senecan plot, *Richard III* does for its
language.[4] The tone of the play is lofty and severely
ornate. Emotional climaxes use a highly stylized language that almost completely obscures individual
voices; but the characteristic appeal of such passages
is to the commonplaces of the family, religion, and
the state, not to literary knowledge. One such moment

is King Edward's lament when he discovers that Clarence is dead:

> Have I a tongue to doom my brother's death,
> And shall that tongue give pardon to a slave?
> My brother kill'd no man: his fault was thought;
> And yet his punishment was bitter death.
> Who sued to me for him? who, in my rage,
> Kneel'd at my feet, and bade me be advis'd?
> Who spoke of brotherhood? who spoke of love?
> (II.i.102-8)

The vocabulary of this speech is by no means Latinate, though it is abstract and generalized. The main poetic devices are rhetorical: parallelism of short clauses and phrases, antithesis, anaphora, and other repetition of key words and ideas. The reiteration of "brother" suggests how unnatural is Edward's crime, how it wars against the love that should bind families together. One hears the natural voice of brotherhood in his recollection of Clarence's words:

> Who told me, in the field by Tewkesbury,
> When Oxford had me down, he rescued me,
> And said "Dear brother, live, and be a king"?
> (111-13)

Their directness and simplicity have the power of contrast in this formally rhetorical speech, but both brothers express reconcilement, the return of natural love. Their reconciliation may be only in death, but their dying words help to evoke the morality by which Richard is finally judged. Reference to the family plays an important part in establishing the moral ground of this passage, as it does in the play as a whole.

Richard himself, who uses the rhetorical patterns of the others only with irony, has a distinctive language in this otherwise homogeneous play. His characteristic idiom is vigorous and homely. Shakespeare may be transferring Sir Thomas More's colloquial irony to Richard, but the device has dramatic precedent in comic morality characters and in the earlier plays of the tetralogy. Anarchic figures like Joan of Arc smile at the formal moralizings of the spokesmen for virtue. Since Richard is the arch-rebel against order, it is not surprising that he excels in parody of the lofty style. The evil that in the Henry VI plays spread through the two conflicting houses of Lancaster and York is by now concentrating more and more in Richard, who acts to destroy his own house and family. Edward, Clarence, Anne, Elizabeth, the Duchess of York—all defend family love and loyalty with at least some sincerity, while he laughs at all such moral claims. Except when the approach of new wars changes the focus of the play for a time, this conflict in attitudes is one of the controlling themes.

Just as in the earlier plays, destruction of the family, corrupted inheritance, and tainted marriage pervade the language and action of *Richard III*. When the Duchess of York recalls what has happened to her family, she sums up the pattern of disorder in the tetralogy:

> My husband lost his life to get the crown;

And often up and down my sons were toss'd,
For me to joy and weep their gain and loss:
And being seated, and domestic broils
Clean over-blown, themselves, the conquerors,
Make war upon themselves, brother to brother,
Blood to blood, self against self.

(II.iv.57-63)

This despair and longing for returned order and natural affection fill most of the characters. Clarence, who repents his earlier ambition, is haunted by a vision of disorder. When his dream inspires remorseful forebodings, he asks that God at least "spare my guiltless wife and my poor children" (I.iv.72). When he disputes with the murderers, he grasps desperately at the hope of Richard's brotherly love and recalls how York charged the three sons to love one another. With similar futility the dying Edward tries to end the quarrels among his kindred and allies and seems to find hope in their hypocritical vows of reconciliation. But when Richard brings the news of Clarence's execution, the king is forced to see the uselessness of his efforts. Even the ordinary citizens are shown worrying about dissension among the new young king's uncles after Edward's death. Only Richard is undisturbed by his awareness of a disorder that has eroded the bonds of family.

The end of the play has a concentration of generalized references to the destruction of the family by civil war and Richard's tyranny. When Richard swears to Queen Elizabeth by the time to come, she denies his right to do so:

The children live, whose fathers thou hast slaughter'd,

Ungovern'd youth, to wail it with their age;
The parents live, whose children thou hast butcher'd,
Old barren plants, to wail it with their age.

(IV.iv.394-97)

As in *3 Henry VI*, this kind of reference helps to expand the significance of the ritualistic scenes of lament. The wailing women become typical of a whole nation, and their tears mark the suffering of England under a curse.

Also the two rivals for the crown appeal to the family in their battle orations, with a characteristic difference of tone. Richmond speaks with lofty abstraction:

If you do fight in safeguard of your wives,
Your wives shall welcome home the conquerors;
If you do free your children from the sword,
Your children's children quits it in your age.

(V.iii.260-63)

The oratory is impeccable with its neatly balanced parallelism and its reliance on stock emotions, but it is rather colorless opposite Richard's bluntness:

If we be conquer'd, let men conquer us,
And not these bastard Bretons, whom our fathers
Have in their own land beaten, bobb'd, and thump'd,
And in record left them the heirs of shame.
Shall these enjoy our lands? lie with our wives?
Ravish our daughters?

(V.iii.333-38)

He appeals to the English heritage of valor and contrasts the corrupted inheritance of the Bretons. The homely vigor of "beaten, bobb'd, and thump'd" plays against the abstract figure of the next line. Apart from its dramatic context, the speech is a fine rallying cry to defend the hearth and home, the sort of words one might expect from Talbot or Faulconbridge. But the last lines are likely to remind the audience that Richard has made "quick conveyance" with Anne (IV.iv.286). He has a legitimate claim to talk of war-like courage, but his appeal to protect the family is blatant hypocrisy.

Richmond has the last word on this theme when in his closing speech he alludes to the family with the power of deeply felt commonplace:

> England hath long been mad, and scarr'd herself;
> The brother blindly shed the brother's blood;
> The father rashly slaughter'd his own son;
> The son, compell'd, been butcher to the sire.
>
> (V.v.23-26)

The link to the father-and-son scene of *3 Henry VI* is apparent, but it is more important that these lines conjure up a vision of all four plays as a time of unnatural disorder, a time now past. E. M. W. Tillyard emphasizes the significance of the oration: "Every sentence of Richmond's last speech, today regarded as a competent piece of formality, would have raised the Elizabethans to an ecstasy of feeling."[5] Though one may find his confidence in the power of commonplace excessive, the judgment is basically sound. In this speech Richmond comes closest to being a worthy antagonist of the formidable Crookback, and his appeal to the family is one source of his strength.

Like family disorder, inheritance is a recurring theme in the language of *Richard III*. Carried over from the earlier plays is the idea of hatred that spreads from parent to child. Richard's enmity is especially quick to go beyond one foe to all his kin, as Elizabeth suggests when she urges her son Dorset to flee because "Thy mother's name is ominous to children" (IV.i.40). Among the other characters Margaret revels in the sufferings of her foes' children. Still this kind of hatred is concentrated more and more in Richard alone. The Duchess of York even tells of having wept for the sufferings of Margaret, who killed her husband and son. And at last virtue can be inherited as well as enmity. The doctrine of orderly succession with its corollary heritage of virtue gradually reasserts itself despite Richard's cynical abuse of it. References to the traditional symbol of the sun-king suggest how powerful a force for good in the land the king is, but at the same time the frequent play on *son* suggests the importance of lineal succession.

Another metaphor of inheritance, that of plants and growth, is even more common. Before Buckingham clearly associates himself with Richard's villainy, he uses this figure to express a noble sentiment at Edward's death:

> Though we have spent our harvest of this king,
> We are to reap the harvest of his son.
>
> (II.ii.115-16)

But as he involves himself in Richard's scheme, the two of them manipulate the ideal of kingly inheritance with cynical freedom. Buckingham learns from his tutor in evil to accuse the new king and his brother of bastardy. In the little play enacted for the mayor and chief citizens, he charges that Richard has abandoned

> The lineal glory of your royal house,
> To the corruption of a blemish'd stock.
>
> (III.vii.121-22)

A few lines later (127) he makes the plant image explicit, and with consummate hypocrisy Richard uses the same image in his rebuff: "The royal tree hath left us royal fruit" (167). But even these cynical echoes reinforce the traditional commonplaces by ironic restatement. They foreshadow the return to orderly succession that Richmond brings.

If Richard is full of expressions of filial duty, Richmond acts like a son. If Richard feigns a tender concern for his mother's name even while blackening it, Richmond asks after his mother with filial concern. If Richard carries his mother's curse into battle, Richmond learns that he has his mother's prayers. Thus the Tudor hero reveals the virtue and strength of a noble inheritance. A shadowy figure he may be, but the ideas he stands for are clear enough. By his marriage to Elizabeth of York he makes the House of Tudor undisputed claimant to the throne (in Shakespeare if not in fact) and therefore untainted in its nobility. For the first time since Edward III's death, hereditary right and the power and ability to rule have come together. Since the threat to successive inheritance has distilled into Richard's malevolence, it perishes with his destruction.

In the Henry VI plays marriage is a tool of ambition and wedded life a microcosm of the disorder in the state. This distortion of the orthodox pattern of marriage recurs in *Richard III,* especially toward the beginning. The folly of King Edward's marriage is an important element in *3 Henry VI,* and in this play Richard echoes all the old attacks on it. Indeed, he suggests that through the queen's rancor the marriage lies behind most of the strife in the court. There is some truth to this charge, since she has apparently used her influence over Edward to elevate her kin, thereby earning the hatred of Edward's family and allies. She seems to have been responsible for Hastings's imprisonment, but of course Clarence's arrest and death, which Richard blames on her, are in fact his own contrivance. There are no women's quarrels at court comparable to that between Queen Margaret and the Duchess of Gloucester in *2 Henry VI,* but there is a hint of similar enmity when Elizabeth alludes to the arrogance of Stanley's wife and Stanley evasively apologizes for her. Here and elsewhere it is not clear how sincere is the queen's avowed meekness and how much it covers spite and ambition for her kin. At any rate, adversity soon drains her of pride, while Richard's rise to power overshadows these petty dissensions of the court.

The most important use of marriage is in the contrast between Richard's Machiavellian schemes and the reconciling union of Richmond and the younger Elizabeth. Seeing in Richmond's marriage a symbol of the reconciliation after the civil war goes back at least to Edward Hall, who in his dedication to Edward VI writes: "For as kyng henry the fourthe was the beginnyng and rote of the great discord and deuision: so was the godly matrimony, the final ende of all discencions, titles and debates."[6] This theme receives its clearest statement in Richmond's closing speech, though it is less trumpeted there than in the ending of *The True Tragedy of Richard the Third,* an anonymous play some form of which was probably one of Shakespeare's sources. The difference is no doubt owing to decorum; it would not be appropriate for this severe tragedy of retribution to end with *The True Tragedy's* pageant of kings and exhortation to England to "kneele vpon thy hairy knee" in thanks.[7] Even so, Richmond's language gives the marriage divine endorsement and cosmic importance:

> Smile Heaven upon this fair conjunction,
> That long have frown'd upon their enmity!
> (V.v.20-21)

Richard as Enemy of the Family

Richard and the women who oppose him determine the role of the family in *Richard III.* Richard's character is established in part by his antagonism toward the values of the family and especially by his behavior toward Margaret, Anne, Elizabeth, and the

Duchess of York. The dramatic role of these women centers in the scenes of lamentation and the episodes of confrontation with Richard which often follow those scenes. Thus one can study the role of the family in the play by looking at Richard's character in relation to it and then at the lamenting scenes and confrontations.

A description of Richard's character in relation to the family is bound to ignore part of him, especially his behavior as politician and warrior. Still much of his character comes out in his dealings with the family. The Richard who dupes the Mayor of London with his prayer book and bishops is not very different from the Richard who convinces Anne of his holy penitence. What loyalty is to the state, love is to the family. In the family as in the state Richard is from beginning to end an alien force, a monster. In his first soliloquy he argues that his hunchback prevents success in love:

> And therefore, since I cannot prove a lover,
> To entertain these fair well-spoken days,
> I am determined to prove a villain,
> And hate the idle pleasures of these days.
> (I.i.28-31)

Shakespeare presents Richard's deformity both ways: as one cause for his hostility to those who can love and be loved and as a portent of his unnatural evil.[8] In an age that has great faith in the power of psychology to explain and eliminate human evil, it is tempting to interpret his malevolence as compensation,[9] but that is oversimple. What makes him formidable and even convincing as a portrait of evil is the discrepancy between the causes for his alienation and the monster he is. Besides, his hunchback is not the only portent that sets him off from ordinary human nature. This play follows *3 Henry VI* in emphasizing his unnatural birth. Not only does the young Duke of York jest about Richard's being born with teeth, but the old Duchess recalls her abnormal birth-pangs in the course of reproving his viciousness. Omens like these have marked him as a demonic force, an enemy to natural order.

In the railing that fills *Richard III*, references to his deformity are countless, but Margaret most accurately defines its symbolic meaning:

> Thou elvish-mark'd, abortive, rooting hog!
> Thou that wast seal'd in thy nativity
> The slave of nature and the son of hell!
> Thou slander of thy heavy mother's womb!
> Thou loathed issue of thy father's loins!
>
> (I.iii.228-32)

Richard is the final corruption of natural inheritance, the extreme result of a process that operates through the entire tetralogy. He has received none of the nobility of the York line, nothing to inspire his parents' pride. Elizabeth charges him with having dishonored his father's death, and his mother repudiates this product of her nurture. Of the many animal images applied to him, which suggest his inhumanity, most important are the frequent references to him as the boar. He inherits, not the symbolic tradition of his family crest, but its literal meaning monstrously come to life. He is not only natural inheritance corrupted ("the slave of nature"), but also a demon incarnate ("the son of hell"). All of the evil that has infected England comes together in one monstrous creature, whose destruction purges the kingdom. The reassertion of family loyalty in others as the play goes on makes Richard's alienation all the more conspicuous.

But Richard is a very special kind of monster, the monster as humorist. To him the code of traditional morality and the bonds of social affection are not a hated enemy but an amusing tool. He uses them to play with other people's emotions, both to attain his secret ends and out of sheer virtuosity. If he were an embittered outcast, he would never have the detachment to be such a consummate hypocrite. Hatred is a powerful form of evil, but Richard goes beyond hatred to the malevolence of the brilliant man, contempt. Without passion he can juggle family affections just as he does religion and political orthodoxy. Every now and then a touch of envy does appear and express itself in open hatred. In the film of *Richard III* Sir Laurence Olivier lets a spasm of rage flash across his face when the young Duke of York playfully refers to his deformity. Buckingham seems to have a glimpse of the power of this hatred when Richard's denial of his suit makes him decide to flee.

This Richard is rarely seen, however. For the most part his dazzling skill in hypocrisy enables him to pose as a supporter of traditional morality. Like the old Vice he is able to manipulate the clichés of family duty; but also like the Vice, when he knows that people see through his hypocrisy, he delights in playing with these clichés simply to shock them. His kneeling for his mother's blessing is a typically sardonic gesture, and it follows close upon the report of an even more cynical piece of deception. Clarence's son tells the Duchess of York that Richard blamed King Edward for Clarence's death, wept, and promised to "love me dearly as a child" (II.ii.26). This trick is the sheer virtuosity of evil, since Richard has no need to dupe this feeble-minded youth. More purposeful though similar in manner are the constant professions of brotherly love to Edward and Clarence.

Richard is also fond of parading the doctrines of moral inheritance. Buckingham and he riot in the pretense that they are shocked by the bastardy of Edward and his sons as well as by Edward's lust and Hastings's adultery with Jane Shore. Buckingham ably picks up the jargon of Richard's pose:

> Withal I did infer your lineaments,
> Being the right idea of your father,
> Both in your form and nobleness of mind.
> (III.vii.12-14)

That is, unlike his supposedly illegitimate brother Edward, Richard is the true inheritor of his father's virtue. Of course Buckingham is no more deceived by these pretenses than Richard himself. Knowing this, Richard delights all the more in playing the tender son who will not have his mother's reputation smeared any more than is necessary. He manipulates the values of marriage just as he does those of filial piety. In seeking an appropriate weapon to oppose the queen's party, he makes great use of Edward's hasty marriage to one of questionable parentage, a widow and a Lancastrian as well.

The flexibility with which Richard changes from pose to pose in the first three scenes, each time expressing a new attitude toward love and marriage, is one of the first indications of his brilliance in villainy. He repudiates love with frank malevolence in the soliloquy that opens the play, but when Clarence enters, a new Richard speaks with soldierly tough-mindedness about Edward's infatuation for his queen and Jane Shore. Like Iago, Richard acts the blunt military man, one who scorns the lust that makes men submit to female dominion. In the soliloquy that ends the scene, this cynicism alters subtly in tone to become, not the public role of rough-spoken virtue, but demonic pleasure in his inversion of all moral standards:

> For then I'll marry Warwick's youngest daughter.
> What though I killed her husband and her father?
> The readiest way to make the wench amends
> Is to become her husband and her father.
>
> (I.i.153-56)

Then, in order to outwit Anne and subdue her weak will, he takes up the role of the conventional Petrarchan lover. A scene later, as he insults the queen and her relatives, he has returned to the blunt soldier, scornful of Edward's uxoriousness and too honest to hide his scorn.

Thus at the beginning of the play Richard's inhumanity allows him to dart from role to role at his pleasure so that he can manipulate the affections and loyalties of the family. His rivals are helpless before him because they are torn between their ambitions and hatreds on the one hand and their scruples on the other. Later he seems to lose power, not so much because he declines as because his opposition is able to find a moral stance. Especially, the murder of the princes, who are his kin and his charge as Lord Protector, unites everyone in shocked opposition. Confronted by this renewed moral unanimity, his hypocrisy is no longer nearly so effective.

With the whole natural order and even the supernatural marshaled against him, Richard momentarily succumbs to horror at his isolation. The coming of the ghosts at V.iii is the last of the emblematic scenes; but of the wailing women only Anne is present, and the family is a minor theme. The soliloquy that follows throws important light on Richard's character. His pride of intellect temporarily suspended by the terrors of the night, he reveals how destructive his chosen isolation from human affection has been:

> I shall despair.   There is no creature loves me;
> And, if I die, no soul will pity me:
> Nay, wherefore should they, since that I myself
> Find in myself no pity to myself?
>
> (V.iii.201-4)

For the first time he feels his isolation with real pain. The last two lines show him regaining control over himself with rueful irony. Only by repudiating pity, even for himself, can he escape the debt of pity for his victims and hence a crippling remorse. This soliloquy is the one occasion on which he speaks of his conscience,[10] and even here Shakespeare's artistry is not especially subtle in portraying his divided mind. Still the moral logic of the passage is clear and true: a man who denies human affection becomes a monster, one in whom even self-love is no more than a tautology: "Richard loves Richard; that is, I am I" (184).

But Shakespeare allows the humorous monster to regain his full vigor before he dies. Richard's return to the battlefield from "this weak piping time of peace" (I.i.24) produces this recovery. If hypocrisy is no longer a possible stance for him, open warfare against the forces of good is. Proclaiming the Machiavel's code, he leads his troops into battle, and Shakespeare gives his great villain a heroic death in single combat with Richmond. Richard dies alone, struggling against the man who will bring order to England, just as he has always stood alone against all the values that bind society together.

The Family as Antagonist

Richard III gives a new prominence to the ritualistic method shown in the father-and-son scene of *3 Henry VI*. In that play Henry VI and two representatives of England lament the consequences of civil war, and in *Richard III* the women lament the victims of Richard's tyranny. The last play of the tetralogy expands the technique into three long passages of ritual grief and several shorter ones. Balancing the pyrotechnic displays of Richard's evil, these scenes reveal the moral force that eventually destroys him. Opposite his fluid rhetoric they establish a severe and lofty idiom, which comes to dominate the play, though at first it may seem ineffective against him. Unfortunately this idiom is strange to modern audiences, so much so that these scenes are severely shortened or eliminated in almost all modern productions, which turn *Richard III* into a one-man play. Sir Laurence Olivier's film version illustrates this tendency.

Such near-unanimity poses the question whether any amount of historical imagination can make these scenes fully effective or whether Shakespeare has simply failed to create a worthy antagonist for his heroic villain. Is Richard too big for his role in the plot, as is often claimed of Falstaff and Shylock? Is his final defeat mere theatrical fakery, called for by the chronicles and a political moral but not given sufficient dramatic cause? Unless nemesis is strong enough to balance the hero-villain, *Richard III* is merely a brilliant melodrama. Since Richmond's role is kept to a minimum, nemesis must speak primarily through the women. Only if these scenes are successful does nemesis have dramatic viability.

Hence Shakespeare has given new importance to his ritualistic scenes. No longer just reiterating an established theme in a different key, they form a vital part of the play. Richmond can oppose Richard as warrior, but this is primarily a play of intrigue, not battle: Richard rises to the throne by plotting against his own family. The women of that family express the values that he opposes, and through the looming presence of Queen Margaret their grief is invested with power. She brings the Senecan power to curse, but she is after all outside the York family and besides is tainted with her own past crimes. She can represent the Senecan vengeance that pursues crime, but not the nobler idea of a ruling Providence. Only when Richard's wife and mother are moved to curse him is his doom sealed. A closer investigation of this pattern in the play may suggest whether or not it succeeds in providing a balance for Richard's villainy.

Lady Anne, widow of a prince whom Richard has helped kill, first sounds the note of lamentation as she follows Henry VI's coffin. Although there is no full-scale scene of mourning, her language foreshadows the later technique. A passage from her monologue illustrates how these lamentations pit Richard's barbarity against the values of the family:

> If ever he have child, abortive be it,
> Prodigious, and untimely brought to light,
> Whose ugly and unnatural aspect
> May fright the hopeful mother at the view,
> And that be heir to his unhappiness!
> If ever he have wife, let her be made
> More miserable by the death of him
> Than I am made by my young lord and thee!
> (I.ii.21-28)

The heavy regularity of the lines, bare of decoration except for their balanced syntax and the paired abstractions, establishes the dominant style for lamentation. But Anne is hardly a formidable antagonist for

Richard, since within two hundred lines she brings this curse on herself.

Richard's entrance violently interrupts her grief, a dramatic pattern that will recur. With remarkable audacity he courts and wins her love. Their language suggests the ease with which he subdues her resistance: Anne is confined to a rigidly formal style, while he slips into and out of whatever artificial mode he chooses. He competes with her in an opening stichomythic combat until he suddenly shatters the decorum (and the meter) with his blunt proposal:

> *Anne.* And thou unfit for any place but hell.
> *Glou.* Yes, one place else, if you will hear me name it.
> *Anne.* Some dungeon.
> *Glou.*   Your bedchamber.
>
>   (I.ii.109-11)

Then with consummate skill he shifts to the Petrarchan language of love. Because he is completely detached from the love and honor that her speech evokes, he can take her out of her depth by using her mode and then suddenly switching out of it. His own characteristic way of speaking reappears with brilliant effect in the soliloquy that closes the scene. This dazzlingly theatrical scene starts one of the central patterns of the play, the confrontation of formal mourning by Richard's amoral virtuosity. Anne's malleability makes the weakness of the women apparent. The consequence of their skirmish is Richard's marriage to his foe's widow, a grotesque parody of the union that ends the play. His anarchic power triumphs with ease over Anne, a representative of traditional values and of the solemn and artificial rhetoric that expresses them.

The first extended scene of wailing comes at II.ii, when the Duchess of York and Queen Elizabeth mourn the deaths of Clarence and King Edward. Clarence's children join in to give the scene an easy pathos, but they also show that the court has not yet come together in opposition to Richard's crimes, that inherited hatreds still divide his enemies. They refuse to mourn Edward because they think that the queen has been their father's enemy. This scene with its antiphony on repeated names and labels of kinship establishes the pattern of communal lamentation.

> *Chil.*   Ah! for our father, for our dear lord Clarence!
> *Duch.*   Alas! for both, both mine, Edward and Clarence!
> *Q. Eliz.* What stay had I but Edward? and he's gone.
> *Chil.*   What stay had we but Clarence? and he's gone.
> *Duch.*   What stays had I but they? and they are gone.
> *Q. Eliz.* Was never widow had so dear a loss!
> *Chil.*   Were never orphans had so dear a loss!
> *Duch.*   Was never mother had so dear a loss!
>
>   (72-79)

The technique is similar to the antiphony of king, father, and son in *3 Henry VI*, though this scene makes less appeal to universal significance and more to pathos. Like the earlier figures, these four are the debris of a conflict that has passed them by, left behind to speak freely because they are so ineffectual.

As with Anne's mourning for Henry VI, the weight of the scene is undercut when Richard enters. He offers a few words of consolation to Elizabeth and then with zestful hypocrisy asks for his mother's blessing. The venerable Duchess obliges him with a blessing that is an implied reproof, but he laughs at her in a flippant aside. He and Buckingham promptly set to work to outwit their rivals, and the scene closes on their scheming. It is clear that their villainy controls events with ease and the women can only register their opposition. Although these women are less malleable than Anne, they are just as futile. The pathos of their mourning may be greater, but there is still no hint that they embody the power of nemesis.

Richard as Machiavellian plotter holds the center of the stage through Act III and the first part of Act IV, though the women appear briefly in II.iv and IV.i. The latter scene shifts abruptly in tone from the triumphant mummery of Buckingham and Richard before the London worthies. Elizabeth, Anne, and the Duchess of York come together to visit the princes in the Tower and there hear the news of Richard's impending coronation. The signs of his hatred and power make their love seem even more futile. Motherly affection can do nothing except harm its children or, worse yet, produce a monster. The Duchess voices this fatal paradox: "O my accursed womb, the bed of death!" (IV.i.53). Anne emphasizes their weakness by recalling how she succumbed to Richard's wooing and how her curse has fallen on her own head. The scene ends with Elizabeth's pathetic lines begging from the Tower itself the humanity of which Richard has stripped the English court:

RICHARD III

Rough cradle for such little pretty ones,
Rude ragged nurse, old sullen playfellow
For tender princes, use my babies well!
(IV.i.100-2)

The conceited epithets for the Tower, which offended
Samuel Johnson,[11] seem appropriate to Elizabeth's
conscious unreality. Like Richard II she indulges her
grief even though she is conscious of her "foolish
sorrow" (103). The tyrant's cynical voice is not allowed to break in on the integrity of this grief, yet his
power is at its peak.

By IV.iv, however, the murder of the princes has
brought a turn of fortune. Margaret now returns to
the action and describes the change vividly:

So! now prosperity begins to mellow
And drop into the rotten mouth of death.
(1-2)

The most powerful of the wailing scenes follows when
the other queens come in to lament the princes' deaths.
Their pathetic vein is toughened by Margaret's more
aggressive rhetoric, in which the iterative imagery of
most early Shakespearian purple passages is just starting to become progressive and organic. (See, for
example, lines 47-58.) Her finest speech, beginning at
line 82, pulls together some of the most important
themes of the play. She recalls the long past history
of crimes that have led to this terrible hour. One line
(86) evokes the image of the Wheel of Fortune,
which raises people up only to throw them down. This

pattern is part of the drama, but later she gives the same figure a different color, one closer to the import of *Richard III*:

> Thus hath the course of justice whirl'd about,
> And left thee but a very prey to time.
>
> (105-6)

Just as in the Tudor modifications of the morality play, Fortune becomes an instrument of retributive justice.[12] With fearsome precision Margaret balances Elizabeth's sufferings against her own, as she has earlier done for the Duchess of York.

Margaret, the only character to appear in all four plays, fuses the events of the tetralogy into a single historical vision. Her tigerish ferocity is not gone but modulated into an austere wrath dignified by the severe regularity of her poetic idiom. She talks with the weight of one who comprehends the whole sweep of events. Thus she surveys the past to show how the destruction of her family has destroyed the families of these rival women. Her force of will inspires them to a new violence of anger against Richard. He is undaunted and apparently unharmed by her curses; after all, she is an old enemy, a Lancastrian. But when the Yorkist women, members of his own family, curse him, his complete isolation becomes clear.

Emboldened by Margaret, the other women sound far less ineffectual when she leaves. As Richard enters in procession, the Duchess of York for the first time pronounces her maternal curse on him. These words are more than "Windy attornies to their client woes"

(127); they imply the strength that is in a curse, a strength that pervades the tetralogy.[13] Richard's mocking tone provides a new confrontation of the two styles, but this time the victory is not unequivocally his. With an admirably orthodox sentiment he calls on drums and trumpets to drown out their agonized questions:

> Let not the heavens hear these tell-tale women
> Rail on the Lord's anointed!
>
> (150-51)

The mock-solemnity is amusing, but his pious words raise the question whether heaven may indeed be hearing their curses. The Duchess, never a contemptible figure, rises to new dignity in this scene, though she cannot silence her son's brisk levity. Even his light answer does not obscure the terrible weight of her question: "Art thou my son?" (155).[14] Now the two strongest-willed people of the drama meet head-on. If Richard is undaunted by her enmity, still his irony is reduced to a petulant "So" by her measured tones.[15]

She leaves the stage and the play with a curse on her unnatural son, one that gains formidable power from its dignity and restraint. Shakespeare uses the Elizabethan horror at a parent's curse to blacken Joan of Arc before her execution, but here the device gains effect from being woven more tightly into the structure of the play. Not only has the curse that leads to retribution been a recurring theme, but this speech foreshadows the ghost scene, in which the souls of Edward's children do, as she prays, curse Richard and bless his foe. It is appropriate that his fortunes turn sharply downward from this point on. Always before his alienation from the human bonds of family has seemed a strength. Now, when his mother's voice merges with nemesis, it becomes for the first time a weakness.

Richard blandly turns from his mother's curse to reenact the wooing scene of Act I. His aim is to guarantee his succession through marrying Elizabeth's daughter. The episode is an extended and less effective version of Anne's courtship, probably in order to suggest his lessening power. His arguments are often perfunctory, as though he were bored with the need to deceive still another foolish woman. He justifies the murder of the princes with a casually brutal remark:

> Look, what is done, cannot be now amended:
> Men shall deal unadvisedly sometimes,
> Which after-hours gives leisure to repent.
>
> (294-96)

It is he who is trapped by an artificial style when in a passage of stichomythy he cannot avoid Elizabeth's bitter jibes, though he does recover his jaunty hypocrisy in the long speech that appears to sway her. Addressing her as "dear mother," that is, his future mother-in-law, is worthy of the early Richard, though the last line of the speech tapers off into petulance.[16]

The proposed match is a second parody-in-advance of the marriage union that ends the play. Richard suggests complacently that only in this way can England be saved. Elizabeth's motives in seeming to accept his offer are not clear, since at the beginning of the next scene Stanley sends word to Richmond that he may have her daughter's hand. The most likely explanation is that she has deceived Richard but that Shakespeare delays this dramatic information briefly. Perhaps he does so in order to keep Richard's decline from being too precipitous. At any rate, the king's ascendancy over the women of the court is no longer so complete as when he was able at will to outwit Anne and reduce Elizabeth, then the reigning queen, to tears. Even his enjoyment of his apparent triumph is thin, a single line of contempt before he turns to other matters.

The whole movement of these confrontations between Richard and the wailing women is from his easy dominance toward slackening of his control. The appearance of the ghosts the night before his death makes even him acknowledge that there is a kind of power he has not taken into account. Then for the first time he feels the strength of nemesis, or rather of Providence, since by this time the moral significance of the force is unmistakable. The ghosts are in one sense projections of his conscience (and of Richmond's confidence), but they are more than that. They speak for a restored moral order, one that has canceled all the bonds that he has himself repudiated. The members of his family, the cast-off confederates of his plots, his old enemies—all turn to Richmond as the king of a new England. Thus the last of the ritualistic scenes makes clear that the order of society has been restored, with Richard cast out.

Conclusion

In his effort to humanize the Senecan dramatic use of nemesis and give it some of the dignity of Christian Providence, Shakespeare makes use of the family, which has already had an important part in the Henry VI plays. Not only do sympathetic characters like the Duchess of York and the dying Clarence evoke the values of the family, but Richard gives them parodic reinforcement by his hypocritical posing. On the whole, the device works. His demonism is shown to stimulate powerful forces that oppose him in the name of love and order. Hence this greatest of villain-kings purges his realm of evil, of the selfish ambition and petty hatreds that have divided the court and laid waste the land. In Seneca, the villains are often mere playthings of fate, swept by passions they cannot control, but Shakespeare's Richard and the nemesis against which he struggles are worthy opposites.

Nevertheless, when in the great tragedies Shakespeare returns to this polarity of love and order versus evil, there is a remarkable deepening of effect. One may recognize Iago or Goneril, Regan, and Edmund as descendants of Richard III even while admiring the increased subtlety and scope; but the love that they try to destroy is embodied in Othello and Desdemona, Lear and Cordelia. It is perhaps an ungrateful question to ask why the characters who embody love are so much less compelling in *Richard III*, but part of the answer is not far to seek. In associating the family with nemesis, Shakespeare gives nemesis some of the immediacy and moral significance of the most basic human institution, but the family also acquires some of the lofty impersonality of Senecan nemesis. It is symptomatic of this development that Richard's language shows extraordinary flexibility, whereas the spokesmen of the family use a stylized, impersonal idiom. The artificiality of their language can be a virtue when it creates a ritualistic movement, one in which the patterned severity of the language suggests the order that Richard tries to destroy. But the family does not come to life as the villainous protagonist does. Richmond is a dramatic nonentity, and even the women are much less distinct as personalities than their enemy.

Confronted with the need to give an impersonal force dramatic equality with a great villain, Shakespeare relies on techniques largely foreign to the modern stage, stylized language and ritualism. If Richard were in any great degree a divided figure, he could himself show the antagonistic force in soliloquy, as Macbeth does. Instead, the earlier Shakespeare uses direct, ritualistic appeal to the traditional sanctions of his world, to the values of religion, the political order, and the family. The voices of the Duchess of York, Richmond, and to some extent even Margaret merge in a lofty expression of these ideals. Richard's variety of language becomes symbolic of anarchy in this world where virtue asserts itself in the austere language of ritual.

However, the moral significance of the contrast may not be so clear as this discussion implies. Defining the forces of *Richard III* in much the same way, Arthur P. Rossiter in a brilliant discussion comes to very different conclusions about their relative morality. His argument is representative of recent attack on the interpretation of the history plays as politically orthodox. Thus he dismisses Tillyard's doctrine of the Tudor myth: "This historic myth offered absolutes, certainties. Shakespeare in the Histories always leaves us with relatives, ambiguities, irony, a process thoroughly dialectical."[17] If this statement meant only that Shakespeare explores the human meaning of political ideas and actions rather than preaching them as do official documents like the *Homilies,* it would be true of the first tetralogy and even more so of the second. But Rossiter goes beyond that to argue that Richard earns a kind of moral approval by his comic detachment and that the operation of Providence as vengeance is deliberately shown as inhumane. If true, both assertions would seriously alter the significance of the family along with the whole dramatic order of the play.

It is true, as Rossiter contends, that until Richard orders the murder of the young princes the full horror of his crimes is blunted by his wit, just as the machinations of the Vice are in the morality plays. Like Jack Cade, Richard is amusing, but to argue that he is therefore good or ambiguous is to confuse aesthetic enjoyment with moral approbation. It is on the face of it plausible that one admires Richard more than his foes when one thinks of his foes as dupes like Anne and Hastings or scoundrels like Buckingham; but is it also true, even for a moment, that a parental blessing is a thing to be sneered at, brotherly love a weakness of fools, and religion a convenient mask? For Richard's humor is the enemy of everything that the Elizabethans found important, and even the twentieth century has not abandoned all these values. The principle of Richard's humor is straightforward: distortion of the normal is amusing when its consequences are not so immediately and visibly painful as to prevent laughter. His hypocrisy is funnier than Zeal-of-the-Land Busy's in *Bartholomew Fair* precisely because the virtues that he apes are real ones, with a genuine claim on the audience.

Rossiter's second argument, that Providence in *Richard III* is inhumane, has even more serious implications. The pattern of crime, curse, and punishment that gives shape to the play is primarily a structural principle, not a description of reality. Nonetheless, it is artistic shorthand for something that Shakespeare, like Hall, must have seen in fifteenth-century England, the vision of a land under a divine curse. The first tetralogy shows an accelerating cycle of evil revenging evil, and surely the orderliness of the progression is not only a literary device. It must imply something about the nature of political disorder. To the extent that Rossiter is asking whether divine mercy is consistent with punishing evil, he raises a question beyond the scope of literary criticism. It is only necessary to remark that it was quite possible for a sane and intelligent Elizabethan to believe in a merciful yet vengeful God.

But Rossiter's argument is vulnerable even within the bounds of dramatic analysis. He neglects to point out what happens to the Senecan chain of nemesis during the course of *Richard III*. Margaret is the voice of nemesis in a cursed land; but as the curse is dissipated, or rather as it is concentrated in the single figure of Richard, she fades out of the play. Richmond and the Duchess of York embody the Providence of a redeemed land, not the nemesis of a cursed land, and they show little of Margaret's sanguinary lust for vengeance. Richmond's oration, the last speech of the play, ends by contrasting the horrors of civil war with peace in a land to which fecundity has returned. The image is of a woman whose wounds are healing—peace or perhaps England—while "the bloody dog" Richard lies dead at Henry Tudor's feet.[18] Life, hope, fertility, a noble young king, a royal marriage on the one hand, and death, the bloody corpse of a villain in whom the sins of a land have perished on the other: surely there is no ambiguity in the choice. *Richard III* dramatizes the triumph of order and justice over the demonic forces released by guilt and civil war, and among the values that share in that triumph is the traditional morality of the family.

[1] Tom F. Driver, *The Sense of History in Greek and Shakespearean Drama* (New York, 1960), pp. 114-15, cautions against uncritical application of the idea of nemesis. In thematic discussion his warning is important, but he underrates the structural similarity between nemesis in Seneca and the impersonal force in this play.

[2] Among the many discussions of Machiavelli and Elizabethan literature are Edward Meyer, *Machiavelli and the Elizabethan Drama* (Weimar, 1897), and Mario Praz, "The Politic Brain: Machiavelli and the Elizabethans," *The Flaming Heart* (New York, 1958), pp. 90-145. On Richard and the Vice figure see Bernard Spivack, *Shakespeare and the Allegory of Evil* (New York, 1958), pp. 386-407.

[3] John Dover Wilson counts 23 classical allusions in *1 Henry VI*, 24 in Part Two, 28 in Part Three, and 7 in *Richard III* (*The Second Part of King Henry VI*, New Cambridge Shakespeare [Cambridge, Eng.,

RICHARD III

1952], p. 1). Virgil K. Whitaker, *Shakespeare's Use of Learning* (San Marino, Calif., 1953), p. 64, has a very different count: in the same order 16, 13, 16, 14. Douglas Bush finds some 50 classical allusions in the three Henry VI plays and only 8 in *Richard III* ("Classical Myths in Shakespeare's Plays," *Elizabethan and Jacobean Studies Presented to Frank Percy Wilson*, ed. Herbert Davis and Helen Gardner [Oxford, Eng., 1959], p. 67). Such are the perils of quantitative analysis. Still, it seems safe to say that most of the allusions in *Richard III* are less conspicuous than those of the earlier plays.

[4] Cf. Wolfgang Clemen, "Tradition and Originality in Shakespeare's *Richard III*," *Shakespeare Quarterly* 5 (1954), 252. On the language of the play see his immensely detailed and thoughtful full-length study, *A Commentary on Shakespeare's Richard III*, trans. Jean Bodheim (London, 1968).

[5] *Shakespeare's History Plays* (London, 1944), p. 201.

[6] *Hall's Chronicle* (London, 1809), p. vii.

[7] Malone Society Reprints, ed. Walter W. Greg (Oxford, Eng., 1929), l. 2206.

[8] Thus Lord Gaspar in Castiglione's *The Courtier* argues that men are ashamed of their deformities "bicause it seemeth by the testimonie of the selfe same nature that a man hath that default or blemishe (as it were) for a patent and token of his ill inclination" (*The Book of the Courtier,* trans. Sir Thomas Hoby, Tudor Translations XXIII [London, 1900], p. 303).

[9] German criticism, following Schlegel, is especially fond of this idea, but the habit goes back to Samuel Johnson, *The Plays of Shakespeare* (London, 1765), V, note on I.i.28.

[10] Anne refers to his "timorous dreams" at IV.i.84. Both passages suggest that Richard is not quite so monolithic as he seems.

[11] See his note at the passage, *Plays*, V.

[12] Cf. Willard Farnham, *The Medieval Heritage of Elizabethan Tragedy* (Berkeley, Calif., 1936), esp. chap. vi.

[13] Thus James I tells his son of the power of a parent's curse: "But assure your selfe, the blessing or curse of the Parents, hath almost euer a Prophetick power joyned with it" (*The Basilicon Doron of King James VI*, ed. James Craigie, Scottish Text Society, 3d. ser., XVI [London, 1944], 155).

[14] Cf. the majestic "Are you our daughter?" which is Lear's first word of reproof to Goneril (I.iv.227).

[15] "If I were playing Richard I would sacrifice anything else in the play sooner than that monosyllable 'So'; which tells more of Richard than a dozen stabbings and baby smotherings" (George Bernard Shaw,

The Star, March 23, 1889, quoted in *Shaw on Music,* ed. Eric Bentley [New York, 1956], p. 266).

[16] "And be not peevish found in great designs." The reading "peevish-fond," repunctuated from "pieuish, fond" in Q1, is rejected by Thompson in the Arden Edition but has a temptingly Shakespearian ring.

[17] "Angel with Horns: The Unity of *Richard III,*" *Angel with Horns and Other Shakespeare Lectures,* ed. Graham Storey (London, 1961), p. 22. For an effective extension of his argument, see Nicholas Brooke, *Shakespeare's Early Tragedies* (London, 1968), pp. 48-79.

[18] Folio and quarto agree in having Richard slain on stage. Stanley's reference to "this bloody wretch" (V.v.5) makes it likely that his body is still there. Since there is no convenient time to remove the body in the brief last scene, it is no doubt carried off at the end as the victors march away. The problem with this explanation is that according to both texts Stanley enters with the crown when Richmond reenters after having killed Richard. If part of the stage direction is mistaken, the detail of the crown seems more likely to be so than the important matter of Richard's death. Or perhaps Stanley is with Richmond when he kills Richard and takes the crown at that time. That, however, seems an undesirable proliferation of stage business. At any rate, the dramatic contrast is the same whether or not Richard's body is actually present to complete the stage picture.

Chapter IV

KING JOHN

I T would be rash to dogmatize about the chronology of Shakespeare's writing, but it is at least convenient to discuss *King John* as an experimental play between the two historical tetralogies. Though *Richard II* is also experimental, it points more directly toward the Henry IV plays, most obviously in its material, but also in dramatic technique. Traditional chronology brings these two plays together in the mid-nineties between *Richard III* and the Henry IV plays.[1] Most critics agree that the verse of *King John* shows a growth in flexibility and power over that of the first tetralogy, though in structure it is not so clearly superior. If, as seems likely, it is Shakespeare's reworking of an earlier play, either *The Troublesome Raigne of King John* (1591) or a common ancestor of that play and Shakespeare's, this disparity is not too surprising.[2]

At any rate, *King John* has dramatic parallels with both *Richard III* and *Richard II*. John shares some of the qualities of the tyrant king, but he also has some of Richard II's vacillation and weakness. Constance's lamentations are not unlike those of the wailing

queens, but they also have the self-conscious prettiness and emptiness of the deposed Richard's speeches.
In one respect *King John* along with *Richard II* dif-
fers markedly from the earlier play. Whereas *Richard
III* counterpoints two styles of poetry, which between
them dominate the language, *King John* is full of the
most diverse kinds of poetic virtuosity. Sometimes the
language has little excuse beyond itself for being in
the play. In such a passage the nobles criticize John's
double coronation with an iteration of poetic figures
that is colorful but finally tedious to modern ears
(IV.ii.1-39).

On the other hand, *King John* does not abandon
the concern of the first tetralogy with order in the
state, and it continues using allusion to the family to
support that theme. Again it shows England turned
aside from the true succession, and again a usurper's
rule reduces the land to chaos. As Faulconbridge
watches Hubert carry young Arthur's body off, he describes what is happening:

> The life, the right and truth of all this realm
> Is fled to heaven; and England now is left
> To tug and scamble, and to part by th' teeth
> The unow'd interest of proud swelling state.
>
> (IV.iii.144-47)

This is a fallen world, one from which Astraea has
fled, to suggest the two myths that lie behind the
passage. Arthur once refers to his era as the iron age
(IV.i.60), and Faulconbridge sums up its morality in
his speech on commodity. When Constance scolds

Queen Eleanor, she uses the doctrine of inherited guilt, that omnipresent theme of the first tetralogy:

> Thy sins are visited in this poor child;
> The canon of the law is laid on him,
> Being but the second generation
> Removed from thy sin-conceiving womb.
> (II.i.179-82)

But most striking about this speech is that it is entirely personal; it is not part of an elaborate pattern of crime and punishment that enfolds the generations. Nemesis does not dominate the language and mood of this play as it did the first tetralogy, especially *Richard III*. There is a moral antithesis between the evil of the usurping John and the good of Arthur, an antithesis that is resolved when Prince Henry succeeds to the throne, supported by the strength and loyalty of Faulconbridge. But neither the good nor the evil attains the compelling dramatic power that both have in *Richard III*. Somehow the moral urgency has gone out of the contrast.

Disorder is still a terrible consequence of the violated succession, and Shakespeare once again uses the family to make its impact vivid. The imagery is full of references to the family as a victim of disorder. When the French king, succumbing to the ethic of commodity, betrays Constance and Arthur, she suggests that all children born on that day will be monstrous. At least in her frenzied imagination, corruption of justice in the state will disrupt the whole order of nature, including the process of generation. King

Philip in a sterner mood alludes to the impact of war
on wives and children (II.i.257), and a French herald
paints a vivid picture as he proclaims a victory for
Arthur:

> Who by the hand of France this day hath made
> Much work for tears in many an English mother,
> Whose sons lie scatter'd on the bleeding ground:
> Many a widow's husband grovelling lies,
> Coldly embracing the discolour'd earth.
>
> (II.i.302-6)

Here the familiar generalized references to the family
are turned into powerful vignettes by the concrete
verbs and adjectives.[3] Instead of the largely verbal
antitheses typical of the earlier style, this passage in-
sists on a visual contrast, the physical reality of the
men's corpses and of the weeping women whom they
have left behind.

Salisbury provides a moving example of the older
rhetoric when, in lamenting the need to rebel against
John, he uses the familiar image of children revolting
against their mother. Later in the same scene Faulconbridge intensifies the same figure to picture the
rebels as "bloody Neroes, ripping up the womb / Of
your dear mother England" (V.ii.152-53). The violence of this figure is typical of the excess in the language of *King John,* which helps to maintain an atmosphere of disorder and corruption extending from
the court to individual men and families. If this kind
of poetry is sometimes more intense and more visually
conceived than in *Richard III,* still it is similar in
structure and purpose.

Like their counterparts in the first tetralogy, these statesmen use marriage as a device in their political schemes. England and France patch up their quarrel through a match between the Dauphin and Lady Blanche, John's niece. Again Shakespeare uses the extravagances of the Petrarchan love idiom to suggest how artificial are the emotions expressed. Hubert proposes the marriage in such language when his motive is entirely to save Angiers from destruction.[4] Both Blanche and Lewis profess their love in the most precious rhetoric. Faulconbridge carries out his role as a choric voice of common sense when he parodies their style and comments directly on the match in his speech on commodity. A sudden interruption, the recurring Shakespearian symbol of the broken ceremony, makes clear the emptiness of this marriage feast. Pandulph's curse on John renews the war between France and England and leaves Blanche to bemoan her dilemma. Unlike Constance, she has no strong personal identity, and so her lamentation falls into a purely conventional pattern:

> Husband, I cannot pray that thou mayst win;
> Uncle, I needs must pray that thou mayst lose;
> Father, I may not wish the fortune thine;
> Grandam, I will not wish thy wishes thrive.
>   (III.i.257-60)

There is no parody in this language, but Shakespeare is content to let the rhetoric fall back on generalized pathos. Blanche is an undifferentiated representative of the women whose loyalties are divided by war, whose marriages are hopelessly corrupted by a world of commodity.

Since this is a play about the royal succession, inheritance is even more prominent than marriage, though Shakespeare is less direct and obvious in using it than the author of *The Troublesome Raigne*. The central issue is the rival claims of John and Arthur (later replaced by Lewis) to be the worthy inheritor of Richard I, the hero-king. John is a tainted heir, a younger brother who has usurped the throne with his mother's connivance. He is an alien figure like Richard III, warring against his own kin to preserve an illegal rule, but John is neither so strong as Richard nor so unequivocally evil. Arthur has moral right on his side, but in his weakness he can hope to achieve the crown only by relying on foreign aid against his own countrymen. He has inherited no more than an empty right, without strength or actual possession. There is a hint of corrupt inheritance in the portrayal of King Philip and Lewis, his son and the would-be heir of Richard I as well. The Dauphin has inherited his father's treachery, though he replaces Philip's spinelessness with the vigor of youth. This base Frenchman's claim to the throne of England is clearly a monstrous perversion of order.

Another prominent use of inheritance is in the quarrel between Lady Faulconbridge's sons, which provides a comic parallel to the main theme of royal succession.[5] It is ironic that John, false holder of the throne, should judge a quarrel over inheritance, one that like his title involves a will and the kin of Richard I. Faulconbridge's history is clearly intended to comment on the issue between John and Arthur, but its implications are not plain. If Faulconbridge parallels John, then his repudiation of his inheritance may contrast with John's attempt to maintain an unrighteous inheritance, or his acceptance of a tainted descent from Richard I may imply that *virtù* is more important than a formally correct title. The ironies of the parallel are not simple like the contrast between the loyal Talbots and the divided court of Henry VI. This technique foreshadows the ironic use of the comic subplot in the Henry IV plays.

Thus *King John* repeats many themes from the first tetralogy, but their significance is seldom so direct and uncomplicated. E. M. W. Tillyard describes the change: "Shakespeare troubles less with what I have called his official self but in redress allows the spontaneous powers of his imagination a freer, if fitful, effusion."[6] In this play the orthodox doctrine of the Tudor myth is still present, but no longer a controlling dramatic principle. As a result, the position of the family as a microcosm of the state, illustrating political issues at a personal level, is less apparent. Shakespeare's art is turning in new directions, though as yet the changes are probing and tentative.

Because its characters are less subdued to any such overriding thematic pattern, *King John* is more psychological than the earlier plays. John approaches being a disinterested study of a tyrant's thinking and behavior, and Constance, Arthur, and Faulconbridge are also of special interest. Since all four of these characters are involved in family ties, the family begins to assume a new, fuller, and subtler role in *King John.*

With Constance and Arthur, Shakespeare mostly expands on the dramatic technique of *Richard III*. Arthur is pathetic in the same vein as the two little princes; Constance is like the Duchess of York in her moral dignity and like Queen Anne in her helplessness. Shakespeare's conception of the mother and son is abstract, based on the idea of right without power. He changes Arthur from a valiant young man to a child and ignores Constance's historical husband (in the latter step following *The Troublesome Raigne*). So modified, they are all the more clearly innocents trapped in a world of commodity and driven to self-destruction. Stopford Brooke describes Constance as "primeval motherhood isolated from everything else in its own passion,"[7] and Arthur is even more simplified as innocent childhood without any distinctive individuality. That they are mother and son is important, yet they have practically no direct contact. Even when they are together, Constance talks past her son in her fiery quarrels for his sake, and he responds to her only by revealing a shy embarrassment at her emotion.

Seizing on a few metaphors from courtly love in Constance's language about Arthur, E. A. J. Honigmann drops an ominous hint about her psychology: "This suggests that a particular fixation was meant."[8] Of course, her hyperbolic grief should suggest madness, since we are later told that she "in a frenzy died" (IV.ii.122). But to seek the cause of her madness in an abnormal attachment to her son is to theorize at random about what Shakespeare has left in shadow. Constance is not a psychologically complete character with incestuous desires and such; she is the apotheosis of maternal love. She and her son speak in an artificial idiom because they are stylized figures, expressive of moral and emotional states rather than idiosyncratic personality. Their only power is verbal, and the artificiality of their language suggests the ineffectuality of such power in a world where King John and King Philip rule.

Mark Van Doren calls Constance "the last and most terrible of Shakespeare's wailing women."[9] His phrase suggests both similarity and difference compared to *Richard III*. Like the women of that play and like Arthur, Constance is a voice of integrity coupled with weakness. The stylized formality of her language suggests idealistic nobility, but also detachment from the cold reality of John's world. Constance is alone in her suffering, surrounded by the embarrassed and fugitive sympathy of a group of cynical men. Cardinal Pandulph's dry comments and King Philip's clumsy ministrations isolate her grief. If the Dauphin seems for a moment to be sympathetic, it soon emerges that his real concern is with the dishonor of losing to the English, and Pandulph quickly ends that concern with his Machiavellian counsel. Counterpointed by such worldliness, Constance's laments cannot develop the symbolic weight of those in the first tetralogy. They cannot expand into a ceremonial antiphony with choric power. On the other hand, her isolation intensifies the pathos of her anguish. Even more than in portraying Arthur, Shakespeare seems to develop the pathos of Constance for its own sake.

According to C. H. Herford, she is "the Juliet of maternal love."[10] Like Juliet she reveals a deeply emotional nature in spite of the artificiality of her poetic idiom. As Arthur's fortunes decline, one sees her austere pride crumble before the overwhelming passion of maternal grief. In her mad scene (III.iii) the ravings of this queenly figure, deprived of husband and son, circle obsessively around marriage and Arthur. The former dominates her opening apostrophe, which shows how the artificial mode can express intense emotion:

> Death! death, O amiable, lovely death!
> Thou odoriferous stench! sound rottenness!
> Arise forth from the couch of lasting night,
> Thou hate and terror to prosperity,
> And I will kiss thy detestable bones
> And put my eyeballs in thy vaulty brows,
> And ring these fingers with thy household worms,
> And stop this gap of breath with fulsome dust,
> And be a carrion monster like thyself:
> Come, grin on me, and I will think thou smil'st,
> And buss thee as thy wife.
>
> (III.iii.25-35)

Here the language of Petrarchan love meets that of the *memento mori*. The fusion begins in the grotesque oxymorons of the second line and extends through the image of death as a bridegroom. The bizarre combination is emphasized by the insistent physicalness of the images and their implicit violence: "And put my eyeballs in thy vaulty brows." Because of these incongruous contents, the ingenuity of the rhetorical patterns becomes perverse.

Constance's sicklied imagination plays with an obsessive image of the human form distorted by time and calamity: the corpse-husband of these lines, and Arthur turned to "a babe of clouts" (58) or so changed by grief that she cannot recognize him in heaven. Half-conscious of her own madness, she says that her grief is the only image of Arthur she has left. Even in her ravings Constance overwhelms the French king and the papal legate by sheer personal force. Her single emotion gives her integrity, that rarest of qualities in this play. But firmness of will merely accelerates her self-destruction in a world where physical strength and cunning alone matter.

Her son is even weaker in the face of wrong supported by brute power. The play leaves no doubt that Arthur is the true inheritor of the crown and John a usurper; Faulconbridge's words over the child's body make that clear. Although there is some suggestion that England's woes spring from the violation of proper succession, the whole theme seems less vital in *King John* than before. Shakespeare is even careless enough to leave Arthur's genealogy in some confusion.[11] King Philip, who can be counted on for proper sentiments if not worthy actions, makes a noble defense of Arthur's right. He contrasts John's "rape / Upon the maiden virtue of the crown" with his rival's honorable title by descent from Geoffrey (II.i.89-109). But Arthur's abstract right has no visible support: a helpless woman is the only representative of his heritage. Hence he is in the impossible position of having to accept aid from Austria, who caused the death of his heroic uncle, Richard I. When Arthur and Austria meet, King Philip refers to "thy unnatural uncle, English John" (II.i.10), "unnatural" because John has stolen the crown from his own kin; but Arthur's alliance with Richard's enemy is also monstrous.

Arthur's most important scene comes after his separation from his mother when his desperate quibbling dissuades Hubert from blinding him. In spite of the artificial, punning style typical of children on the Elizabethan stage, the scene creates a simple but powerful pathos. Arthur tries even to repudiate his parentage in an appeal to the evil-looking Hubert's sympathy:

> Is it my fault that I was Geoffrey's son?
> No, indeed, is't not; and I would to heaven
> I were your son, so you would love me, Hubert.
> (IV.i.22-24)

One is reminded of Henry VI wishing that he were a shepherd rather than a king and the widowed Queen Elizabeth promising to slander her daughter's birth in order to save her from Richard III. Hubert responds to the claims of Arthur's weakness and innocence, the claims of affection that King John has ignored.

Despite this victory over his uncle's malice, Arthur is too weak to survive. He jumps to his death during a futile attempt to escape. It is ironic that the first disinterested support of his claims, the nobles' rebellion, comes just too late to be of any use.[12] As the murder of the princes in the Tower rallies England against Richard III, so Arthur's death marks the turning-point in John's fortunes. Both episodes evoke similar pathos and rely on the same artificial rhetoric. But John is less clearly guilty than Richard III, and the chain of moral causation that leads to his downfall is perfunctorily developed. There is no overwhelming tide of familial and political indignation that carries John to his death. Faulconbridge, whose views are by now the main moral guide of the play, supports him, though with reluctance.

There are close parallels between Shakespeare's John and Richard III as politicians, as warriors, and as conspirators against their own families, as this discussion has already suggested. Shakespeare ignores the Protestant effort to whitewash John as a heroic opponent of Catholic interference, a tendency somewhat more prominent in *The Troublesome Raigne* and central to John Bale's *Kynge Johan.*[13] In defying France, John expresses the sentiments of Tudor orthodoxy (Shakespeare's villains often do), and there is some inconspicuous anti-Catholic or at least anti-clerical satire centering on Cardinal Pandulph. Nevertheless, this John is primarily the villain-king, a foe of order and succession who sacrifices England's welfare to his own position. His unconcern for the bonds of family shows plainly enough in his treatment of Arthur. Though he is upset when Hubert reports Arthur dead, that is merely because the murder has turned out to be harmful to his interests. Occasionally he shows the brilliant delight in evil of Richard Crookback himself. Thus, when Arthur is captured, he feigns an uncle's love while hiding his real intent behind a sardonic pun:

Thy grandam loves thee; and thy uncle will
As dear be to thee as thy father was.

(III.ii.13-14)

Yet for all their similarities, John is a very different
character in a very different play.

Both John and Richard are alien creatures, void of
normal human feelings; but whereas Richard's alienation seems an act of his will that leaves him able to
play with others' feelings, John seems rather a dwarfed
human being. He is unable to exploit men with complete ruthlessness because he lacks Richard's monolithic single-mindedness. Despite his considerable military and political abilities, which the early scenes reveal, he is unable to stand alone. His impulsive ac-
tivity masks a lack of will. When he can no longer
depend on his mother's strength, he reacts to his opposition with sporadic outbursts that do little except
antagonize his supporters. In despair he turns the
whole conduct of the war over to Faulconbridge, and
Shakespeare dismisses him from the play with almost
contemptuous haste, poisoned by a monk and raving
in a way that recalls the madness of his enemy, Constance. There is something appropriate in the death
of this sin-crippled man, obsessed with the poison in
his vitals, unable even to perceive the affectionate sorrow of those around him.

The best thing about John is the love that he moves
in Prince Henry and Faulconbridge. Selfish and inar-
ticulate though he is, he has a rough fondness for
those closest to him that earns their loyalty. He is
genuinely fond of his mother and dependent on her

advice, as his aimlessness after he leaves her in France suggests. When he hears of her death, his first reaction is a selfish concern with the state of his French territories, but some fifty lines later he is still brooding on the news: "My mother dead!" (IV.ii.181). If he has no real feeling for his nephew, at least he has some scruples about ordering his death. In the much-praised scene in which he arranges for the killing, it is not Hubert whom he is persuading; it is himself.

Faulconbridge's rough-hewn good nature stirs John to his closest personal warmth, even to submissiveness. It is as though he were still subservient to his brother's heroic personality, now reincarnate in Richard's illegitimate son. Early in the play he can reprove Faulconbridge's levity with kingly dignity (III.i.60), but he finally hands over to the Bastard his generalship, his strongest claim to personal significance. It is ironic that John's few affections come out as vacillation and submissiveness, the yielding of a weakly evil man. He is a very different version of the traditional dramatic tyrant-usurper. By showing him as son, uncle, and father, Shakespeare has probed more deeply into his psychology than by similar means with Richard III. If the second handling gives a less compelling stage figure, it is also more recognizable as a human form of evil.

In Faulconbridge, the main choric figure, Shakespeare turns to the symbolism of bastardy, but the meaning of the symbol is by no means clear.[14] Bastardy in Elizabethan lore is a sign of moral depravity. By this tradition Faulconbridge should be the epitome of England's decline, a representative of how John's usurpation has corrupted the state. But in fact his Machiavellianism is of a singularly unconvincing sort. He plays at deep policy, but in real conflicts of principle he acts uniformly on the basis of loyalty to the king, first John and then his heir. His main role is in the quasi-pastoral tradition of satiric comment on the court by a naïve but realistic observer from the country. He is the bright country squire who comes to the court, learns its ways, and comments shrewdly on the decadence that he sees. Just as his political significance does not fit the patterns of stage Machiavellianism, so the tag of bastardy does not describe his whole relationship to the family. Shakespeare complicates the symbolism with considerable subtlety.

John F. Danby describes Faulconbridge's symbolic place: "Broadly speaking, Shakespeare's problem is how to legitimize the illegitimate."[15] He argues that *King John* reveals Shakespeare's abandonment of the theological framework of the first tetralogy for a benign Machiavellianism. That might be so if Faulconbridge were to become king, but there is no suggestion of any such possibility.[16] On the contrary, he supports orthodox succession in Prince Henry's title, though when John was king *de facto*, Faulconbridge supported him with equal loyalty. Hence his bastardy is not a symbol that defines his whole being, only part of a complex figure. Shakespeare is not content to rely on the stock emotions of a tag like "bastard" any more than he does on those of "Jew" in Shylock. In the corrupt world of *King John*, Faulconbridge embodies the highest good available. He combines clear-eyed insight into unscrupulous politics with a deeply idealistic

KING JOHN

patriotism. Even *The Troublesome Raigne* is able to
rise above the crudities of stock response to bastardy,
but Shakespeare goes far beyond his predecessor in
creating a psychologically convincing moral commentator for his play.

Looking at the externals of the play, one can make
a case for him as another Jack Cade, a representative
of the New Men who try to rise above the station in
life prescribed by medieval orthodoxy. Faulconbridge
advances himself by supporting a usurper; Cade hopes
himself to replace the reigning king. Both men mock
the forms that uphold tradition, especially ceremony
and religion. Cade repudiates his parentage, and Faulconbridge denies that his mother's husband was his
father. Indeed, he undercuts the whole Elizabethan
doctrine of inheritance with words that echo Richard
III's declaration of moral self-sufficiency: "And I am
I, howe'er I was begot" (I.i.175). From this point of
view there is a terrible irony in the fact that John steals
the throne from his legitimate nephew and drives him
to his death, only to make this bastard nephew the
most powerful man in England. Because John's usurpation has corrupted orderly succession in the realm, men
like Faulconbridge and Hubert rise while the nobles
are forced into rebellion. One might conclude that
Faulconbridge is the bastard as natural man, one
whose base impulses lack ethical restraint.

However, the ethical pattern of *King John* is not
that simple. As John Dover Wilson remarks, "The
B[astard] is a kind of obverse to Richard III; Richard
is always telling us he is determined to prove a villain
and proves one; Faulconbridge is always proposing to

follow the way of the world and fights for a losing cause."[17] His decision in the first scene can be viewed in quite a different light. After all, Richard I was in fact his father, and so in taking his name, he is really accepting his parentage, not denying it. As Honigmann's note points out, Eleanor tests his moral inheritance before accepting him as her grandson and ally, and he passes the test when he displays the cavalier boldness of his father.[18] He completes the proof that he is heir to Richard's courage by killing Austria and going on to become the mainstay of the English army and John's rule.

Besides, it is not fair to call him cruel to his mother. His filial piety may seem unusually frivolous, but that is because he invariably hides his affections behind flippancy. Even to the formidable Queen Eleanor his gratitude and respect are tinged with impudence. Also he treats his mother with some kindness in their brief interview, in contrast with the same episode in *The Troublesome Raigne*, where he rantingly threatens to kill her in order to discover his father's name. In *King John* he bullies and teases her into revealing her shame, but only after getting James Gurney out of the way. Finally, he undertakes to defend her honor from the world, though with a characteristically irreverent pun in his last word (on "naught," meaning "naughty"):

> If thou hadst said him nay, it had been sin;
> Who says it was, he lies: I say 'twas not!
> (I.i.275-76)

Thus from another point of view Faulconbridge, like Alexander Iden, is a representative of the deep-rooted virtue that emerges to save England when its leaders seem hopelessly weak or corrupt. He demonstrates that the heroic tradition of Richard I is not dead even in the new world of commodity. His bluntness is opposed less to ceremony itself than to pretended ceremony and artificial rhetoric, the hypocrisy of a degenerate society. He sneers at the Dauphin's love language because the marriage is obviously one of convenience,[19] but he does not sneer at Arthur's title to the crown. Just as he is loyal to his mother and Eleanor while avoiding the cant of devotion, so he defends the established order with his blunt speech and his strength. There is nothing metaphysical about his conservatism, no speeches on order among the bees or the divine right of kings. Like the keepers who take Henry VI prisoner (*3 Henry VI*, III.i), he supports the established order, the reigning king, no matter what the king's faults may be. Shocked though he is at Arthur's death, he never doubts where his loyalty should rest, and the play supports his choice. The rebels turn out to be aiding French domination of England, and Faulconbridge's loyal defense allows the noble Prince Henry to succeed to the throne with undisputed title.

Faulconbridge is indeed one of the New Men. Of equivocal birth, he establishes a place for himself by his valor and efficiency, his *virtù*. But he never really violates the order of his society. Above all, he never commits the worst of political sins, rebellion. His is the conservatism of common sense, just as his love for his mother does not blind him to the fact that the uncertainty inherent in paternity may apply to his father. He makes an ideal commentator for this play because he is resolutely loyal and yet without illusions. Shakespeare could not afford this kind of commentator in the first tetralogy, where the moral polarity is tidier; but in this play of half-hearted villainy and ineffectual good, the blunt choric figure of Faulconbridge is so useful that he steals the center of the stage from his betters, even from King John.

Conclusion

King John is a rich but untidy play. No one theme or character dominates it as the theme of order and disorder controls the first tetralogy and the title character dominates *Richard III*. In structure John is clearly at the center of the play, but, if anything, Faulconbridge comes closer to holding the center of attention. Again Shakespeare portrays a world corrupted by the violation of proper order, but this view is less desolate than in the first tetralogy. A world governed by commodity is no doubt less desirable than a world of perfect order, but at least it is recognizable as rather like our own. It is not the demon-ruled England of *Richard III*, not even the chaos of the Henry VI plays. If the violent evil of those plays is less conspicuous in *King John*, so is the severe ordering of events that compels evil to destroy itself and good to triumph. Instead of the titanic war between Richard III and nemesis, there are only equivocal figures like King John, the wavering tyrant, and Faulconbridge, the baseborn hero.

KING JOHN

Shakespeare has cast off the rigid quasi-Senecan order of the first tetralogy. His new freedom has resulted in growing complication of the characters, who thereby become more interesting; but what traces of shape the play has are left over from the pattern of *Richard III*. John is the villain who struggles against the forces of order and is defeated, to be replaced by a monarch who returns to order and due succession. But the moral urgency has gone out of this contrast; it does not govern the details of *King John* as it does those of *Richard III*. Among other elements the family loses its clarity of function even while gaining new richness and variety.

---

[1] Peter Alexander and others have argued for about 1590 as the date of *King John,* though Alexander would put the whole first tetralogy back into the 1580s, thus preserving the orthodox order. See a tentative passage in *Shakespeare's Life and Art* (London, 1939), p. 85, and *Shakespeare's Henry VI and Richard III* (Cambridge, 1929), pp. 193-215. E. A. J. Honigmann in his New Arden Edition (Cambridge, Mass., 1954) argues for "the winter/spring of 1590/91" (p. lviii). The evidence for that date is not very compelling, but neither are the arguments for 1596 or any other date. If on internal grounds one is inclined to believe *King John* later than the first tetralogy, it is almost impossible to decide whether it precedes or follows *Richard II*, though the continuity of narrative makes it natural to associate the latter play with the second tetralogy. Once again, references to these plays that imply an order of composition should be taken as a matter of convenience in writing, not a necessary presumption of the analysis.

[2] Following Alexander's hint, Honigmann argues that *The Troublesome Raigne* derives from *King John* rather than the other way around (pp. liii-lviii, Appendix B). He raises a few points difficult to explain on the older assumption that *John* is based on *The Troublesome Raigne* in its present form, but he does not overcome the far greater difficulties of his theory. Without going through the very complex arguments here, I will proceed on the assumption that, if *King John* is

not derived from *The Troublesome Raigne,* it comes from a source-play rather like *The Troublesome Raigne.* Since such a play is unlikely to have been by Shakespeare, it will not distort the probable truth too much to refer to *The Troublesome Raigne* as one of his sources.

[3] Samuel Johnson praises the passage, although he finds the image of the husband embracing the earth altogether too strong. Quoted in New Variorum Edition, ed. H. H. Furness Jr. (Philadelphia, 1919), n. at II.i.319 (hereafter cited as New Variorum).

[4] I follow my source-text, Honigmann's edition, in assuming that Shakespeare intended to merge the parts of the Citizen and Hubert. It is possible that the two parts were simply taken by the same actor.

[5] The basis for this parallel exists in *The Troublesome Raigne,* although Shakespeare changes its whole tone by his handling.

[6] *Shakespeare's History Plays* (London, 1944), p. 218.

[7] *Ten More Plays,* p. 245, quoted in New Variorum, p. 585.

[8] Note at III.iii.104.

[9] *Shakespeare,* Anchor Books (Garden City, N.Y., n.d.), p. 91.

[10] Quoted in New Variorum, p. 633.

[11] See especially the problem at II.i.177, where Constance describes Arthur to Eleanor as "thy eldest son's son."

[12] William H. Matchett, "Richard's Divided Heritage in *King John,*" *Essays in Criticism* 21 (1962), 244-46, argues that the nobles are not disinterested, as their previous correspondence with the Dauphin proves. However, there is no hint that this correspondence precedes the break with John, and Salisbury's grief at having to revolt (V.ii.11-39) has the ring of truth. James L. Calderwood, "Commodity and Honour in *King John,*" *University of Toronto Quarterly* 29 (1960), 345-47, agrees with Matchett, but his reading demands a retrospective irony untrue to any impression in the theater.

[13] Bale's morality play is a rigidly Protestant propaganda piece dating about 1538 in its original form. There is no evidence that Shakespeare knew this play, and it survived only in manuscript until the nineteenth century.

[14] Indeed, John W. Draper, *Stratford to Dogberry* (Pittsburgh, 1961), p. 63, denies that the characteristics of bastardy are relevant to Faulconbridge since he is by law and custom legitimate. The point seems strained, since even Faulconbridge's mother admits that Richard I is his real father.

[15] *Shakespeare's Doctrine of Nature* (London, 1949), p. 75.

[16] Matchett's article argues the contrary, but he is stretching the text, especially when he contends that Hubert implicitly offers the

crown to Faulconbridge in V.vi. Again Calderwood anticipates his argument.

[17] *King John,* New Cambridge Edition (Cambridge, Eng., 1936), p. 131, note to II.i.598. For a closer association of Faulconbridge, Richard III, and the bastard Edmund, see Ronald Berman, "Anarchy and Order in 'Richard III' and 'King John'," *Shakespeare Survey* 20 (1967), 51-59.

[18] Note at I.i.135.

[19] In *The Troublesome Raigne* Faulconbridge is jealous of the Dauphin because Blanche has been promised to him. Shakespeare eliminates this motive, perhaps in order to maintain the Bastard's sardonic detachment.

Chapter V

RICHARD II

TILLYARD finds more of Shakespeare's "official self" in *Richard II* than in *King John*—more of the ceremonial language and ritualism that underscore the political theme of the first tetralogy.[1] The family shares in this return to an older technique. Many themes of the earlier plays recur in much the same mode, though, as *King John* has already shown, the growth of Shakespeare's poetic skill gives them a new intensity of coloring. Richard's deposition begins a cycle of guilt and punishment that ends only with the triumph of Henry Tudor at the end of *Richard III*. As a result, it is natural that this play should emphasize the prospect of a chain of inherited guilt that will destroy the whole order of the kingdom.

Just before the deposition the Bishop of Carlisle closes a powerful statement of monarchical orthodoxy with a prophecy:

> The blood of English shall manure the ground,
> And future ages groan for this foul act,
> Peace shall go sleep with Turks and infidels,
> And, in this seat of peace, tumultuous wars

Shall kin with kin, and kind with kind, confound.
Disorder, horror, fear, and mutiny,
Shall here inhabit, and this land be call'd
The field of Golgotha and dead men's skulls—
O, if you raise this house against this house,
It will the woefullest division prove
That ever fell upon this cursed earth.
Prevent it, resist it, let it not be so,
Lest child, child's children, cry against you woe.
                                                    (IV.i.137-49)

Unlike Richard's anguished prophecies, this is a purely
impersonal utterance, parallel to the choric speeches
of the first tetralogy. The first line prepares for the
whole passage by uniting the two main senses of
"blood," the sign of inheritance and of death. Latent in
the image is the terrible paradox of death, the most
sterile of things, as fertile and breeding.[2] Such poetic
compactness is rare in the earlier plays, but the broad
sweep of phrases like "kin with kin" and "child, child's
children" is typical of the generalized references to
destruction of the family in the Henry VI plays. The
biblical phrasing of the ninth line (145) suggests the
kind of radical disorder that Christ envisages, going
beyond the rival families of Lancaster and York to "this
cursed earth," the kingdom, and indeed all of fallen
humanity. Such allusions are less common in *Richard II*
than in the first tetralogy, but they still have their place.

The most prominent family theme, indeed one of the
main threads of the play, is inheritance.[3] *Richard II* is
in part a drama of fathers and sons, not only in its
emphasis on orderly succession, but also in its study
of moral inheritance. The opening two scenes establish

the theme in two different keys. In the first it appears
in a setting of splendid pageantry and public utterance,
but the second scene is a deeply emotional private discussion. The immediate impression of the opening
scene is of chivalric heroism with two knights defying
each other in the finest oratorical vein. Mowbray and
Bolingbroke repeatedly call on the traditional association of heroic courage and honor with noble birth, the
great Renaissance tradition of aristocratic idealism.
Bolingbroke touches on this idea in his first defiance:

> Thou art a traitor and a miscreant,
> Too good to be so, and too bad to live,
> Since the more fair and crystal is the sky,
> The uglier seem the clouds that in it fly.
>
> (39-42)

That is, Mowbray is "too good," too wellborn, to be a
traitor; a base nobleman is so unnatural as to have
forfeited his right to live. Mowbray shows proper respect for the king's blood in his enemy, but with
Richard's permission returns the charges of "this
slander of his blood" (113). When Bolingbroke refuses to withdraw his challenge, he suggests the son's
duty to emulate his father in courage: "Shall I seem
crest-fallen in my father's sight?" (188).

The most serious charge that Bolingbroke brings
against Mowbray is the murder of Gloucester, Bolingbroke's paternal uncle. Hence his challenge is an act of
filial piety, vengeance for his injured family. He refers
to his uncle's blood:

Which blood, like sacrificing Abel's, cries
Even from the tongueless caverns of the earth
To me for justice and rough chastisement;
And, by the glorious worth of my descent,
This arm shall do it, or this life be spent.

(104-8)

He sees his pursuit of revenge as a sign of his noble
birth. But his comparison of Gloucester and Abel suggests that there is another side to all this splendid
pageantry, since Abel was killed by one of his own
family. Clearly the reference is a veiled attack on the
king himself, who is ultimately responsible for his
uncle's death.[4] For all his public stance of impartiality
and feudal correctness, Richard has shed the blood of
his own family; the judge is an unnamed defendant.

Just as Richard's position is equivocal, so is Bolingbroke's. His arrogation to himself of the duty to dis-
pense justice is presumptuous in the presence of his
king, however guilty that king may be; Gaunt's declaration of Tudor orthodoxy in the next scene makes that
clear. Richard is moved to a veiled reproof of his
cousin's boldness even while proclaiming his impartiality:

Were he my brother, nay, my kingdom's heir,
As he is but my father's brother's son,
Now by my sceptre's awe I make a vow,
Such neighbour nearness to our sacred blood
Should nothing privilege him nor partialize
The unstooping firmness of my upright soul.

(116-21)

On the surface this speech is a fine public display of impartiality, but behind it is a double irony. Richard dwells with conscious sarcasm on the names of kinship that locate Bolingbroke, a mere cousin of the king in spite of his presumption. He is denying the significance of Edward III's blood in Bolingbroke and hence the basis of his own royalty, whereas in a later scene Northumberland affirms "the royalties of both your bloods" (III.iii.107) even while plotting against Richard. Neither man accepts the full implications of the orthodox values he evokes.

Hence it is already clear that Richard is not impartial and cannot afford to be in the face of an attack on his sovereignty. But there is a second, unconscious, irony in the words, for this upstart is soon to prove "my kingdom's heir" indeed. The lines foreshadow Richard's bitter play on the same relationships as he surrenders to Bolingbroke's power:

> Cousin, I am too young to be your father,
> Though you are old enough to be my heir.
> (III.iii.204-5)

It is significant that Bolingbroke defies his father's command to throw down Mowbray's gage. He visibly rebels against his duty as a son just as he later will against his duty as a subject. All the spectacle and rhetoric in the first scene only partly cover a grave disorder in the state, and the theme of inheritance is closely involved with both spectacle and disorder.

If on the surface this scene illustrates proper inheritance of courage and loyalty, the second reveals a dilemma of conscience typical of a disordered state. John of Gaunt and his brother's widow debate whether his duty to Gloucester, his brother, outweighs his duty to the king. The duchess defends the family in a set piece on the sons of Edward III (9-36), which alternates metaphors of blood and a growing tree, the standard images of the family. She sees the claim of family unity as absolute:

> Yet art thou slain in him; thou dost consent
> In some large measure to thy father's death
> In that thou seest thy wretched brother die,
> Who was the model of thy father's life.
>
> (25-28)

To our ears her charges may seem the conceits of frenzy, but the weighty simplicity of her lanuage suggests that more is involved. In the ordered universe of orthodox vision, the family is a union of supernatural power, part of the whole order of being. In a magical sense the son is indeed the father reincarnate. Gloucester's spilt blood is a physical sign of the noble inheritance in the House of Lancaster. For Gaunt to omit vengeance is to deny his birth, to commit the sin of despair in the name of patience (29-34). Gaunt does not deny the validity of her arguments. His words acknowledge "the part I had in Woodstock's blood" (1), but appeal to what he considers an even more basic principle than family loyalty, the sanctity of the king. Gaunt argues that in a deeper sense he lives up to his birth by his submission. He shows that Edward III's sons have not forgotten their prime duty of loyalty to the English monarch, the head of their family. Brother of one great warrior and son of another, he is the last full inheritor of their heroic virtue.

For this theoretical debate Shakespeare has both characters use severely impersonal rhetoric, but he gives emotional reality to the duchess's affection for her brothers-in-law with a sudden shift in tone. Their argument left unsettled, the lonely widow tries fondly to keep Gaunt from leaving so quickly and voices her longing to see York. Shakespeare is no longer satisfied to leave even a nonce-character like her a purely impersonal voice. At the same time as he works the verse into formal conceits, he manages to express the broken accents of grief in a way that shatters the rigid formality (58-74). Even so, the main function of the scene is to establish John of Gaunt's role of aged wisdom. In a demonstration of the noblest orthodoxy, he is prepared to sacrifice the dearest ties of kinship and love to the ideal of political order, which both his son and his nephew violate.

The first two scenes of *Richard II* have several important functions. They establish the theme of inheritance as a major one. They make clear that behind the ceremonial pomp of the state is a disorder that creates painful conflicts of duty. They begin a contrast between what seems to be happening and what really is, between proclaimed purpose and hidden motive, between word and deed. Finally, they make John of Gaunt a standard against which his son and nephew are measured. As the play develops, the family theme centers on three figures—the Duke of York, Bolingbroke, and Richard himself.[5] Analysis of these three in their family relationships should indicate the direction that Shakespeare's art is taking.

For most of the play the Duke of York has a straight-forward role. He is a weaker John of Gaunt, one who voices all the right sentiments, but lacks the will to carry out his good intentions. When Richard confiscates Gaunt's estates, York protests in words that predict the whole course of events:

> Take Herford's rights away, and take from time
> His charters, and his customary rights;
> Let not to-morrow then ensue to-day:
> Be not thyself. For how art thou a king
> But by fair sequence and succession?
>
> (II.i.195-99)

To violate succession, the outward equivalent of moral inheritance, is to deprive a man of his place in society and hence of his very identity, as Richard is to discover.[6] But York cannot act on this wisdom, nor can he oppose the rebel Bolingbroke despite his bold "I am no traitor's uncle" (II.iii.87). York is the last of Edward III's seven sons, a fading remnant of the old order. In this new order in which there is no simple duty, no clear object of loyalty, he is an anachronism. Like Humphrey, Duke of Gloucester, and that other Gloucester in the anonymous play *Woodstock*, he fails as a statesman through a too-innocent goodness, one that cannot cope with the power politics of a degenerate age.

At the end of the play York transfers his loyalty to the new Henry IV as king *de facto*, having convinced himself that Richard's voluntary deposition is valid. However, since his son Aumerle is Richard's zealous supporter, York is caught in another dilemma of loyalty. When he discovers that Aumerle has joined a plot against the king, he threatens to denounce his son and does so. If York's determination here seems to contradict the established impression of his vacillating character, perhaps it is because Shakespeare indulges in rather frivolous self-parody, what R. F. Hill calls "a kind of savage farce."[7] Often before he has created scenes of stylized emotion using couplets, stichomythy, and abstract language. Even in this play Gaunt expresses just such a dilemma of loyalty as York's in stiffly formal couplets (I.iii.236-46). But nowhere else has the dignity of the technique been so undermined by comic bathos. While York rages at his son's treachery, he calls angrily for his boots. The duchess caps a noble appeal to the pains of childbirth with a housewifely proof of her son's legitimacy:

> He is as like thee as a man may be,
> Not like to me, or any of my kin.
>   (V.ii.108-9)

Finally, so that Aumerle may hasten to get the king's pardon, his mother proposes that he steal York's horse.

The confrontation before the new king at first seems serious enough. In nobly metaphorical language Henry expresses the traditional shock at vice descended from virtue, a muddy stream sprung from a silver fountain (V.iii.58-61). But with the arrival of the duchess he comments, "Our scene is alt'red from a serious thing"

157

(77), as he drops into the prevailing couplets. From now until the speech with which he closes the episode, Henry is almost as taciturn as in the deposition scene; but his countenance, varying between anger and amusement, governs the tone. The old-fashioned style of this dispute is as out of place in the usuper's court as is York's anachronistic virtue. Both are objects of laughter to the generous but pragmatic king. It is as though Shakespeare were bored with the easy success of a stylized dilemma-scene. The Duke of York amuses him too much to be taken seriously in a tragic conflict of loyalty between son and king.

The shadowy figure of Bolingbroke is shown both as son and as father, the latter only briefly in this play. He is a somewhat colorless figure so as not to compete with Richard in dramatic interest, but Shakespeare turns this technical necessity into a point of characterization. At moments of crisis he is taciturn, Richard's "silent king."[8] Although he is not without eloquence, there is always an element of calculation to his rhetoric, as though the reality were something colder and harder that lay behind his words. Shakespeare makes this quality clear by contrast with his father, that magnificently conventional figure. His virtue established in the first two scenes, John of Gaunt acts as another of the idealized old counselors of the king, like Eubulus in *Gorboduc*. On his deathbed he expresses the political ideal of the play in the accents of public rhetoric. "Like a prophet new inspir'd" (II.i. 31), he denounces his nephew's crimes:

O, had thy grandsire with a prophet's eye

Seen how his son's son should destroy his sons,
From forth thy reach he would have laid thy shame,
Deposing thee before thou wert possess'd,
Which art possess'd now to depose thyself.

(II.i.104-8)

Behind the elaborate wordplay is Gaunt's sense of
Richard's unnatural and self-destructive attack on his
family, the roots of his being. The clearest dramatic
representation of Richard's guilt and the act that
ensures his deposition is the betrayal of this old man's
loyalty by seizing his estates. As he appeals to the
traditional sanctions of family and state, Gaunt's
poetry is laden with the abstract eloquence characteristic of virtue in the first tetralogy.

As Richard relies on his inherited right against the
usurper's threat, so Bolingbroke with scrupulous piety
cites his inheritance from this great father:

O thou, the earthly author of my blood,
Whose youthful spirit in me regenerate
Doth with a twofold vigour lift me up
To reach at victory above my head,
Add proof unto mine armour with thy prayers.

(I.iii.69-73)

But both members of the new generation have lost
touch with the meaning behind their words. Although
Gaunt gives Bolingbroke his blessing, his son has de-
fied both him and their king in pressing the quarrel
with Mowbray. Still Shakespeare is careful not to turn
his future king into an unredeemed rebel or a pure
Machiavel.[9] Bolingbroke is a chastened figure when

159

Richard announces his banishment, and the grief of his parting from father and homeland seems real enough. But later, when his uncle York chastises his rebellious return to England, he shows his glib mastery of the language of filial piety. With sincere feeling he argues his right of inheritance, which is legitimate, but he also plays on York's emotions:

> You are my father, for methinks in you
> I see old Gaunt alive.
>
> (II.iii.116-17)

York is able to sort out the valid from the specious in his nephew's plea, though he lacks the power and will to act on his knowledge. No doubt Bolingbroke's pride in his inheritance is real, but most of his public appeals to the bonds of family are mere rhetoric at the service of practical ends.

At least in *Richard II* Bolingbroke is the master of this contrast between verbal tribute to family ideals and the reality of power politics. Deprived of his proper inheritance from the noble John of Gaunt, he makes himself seem to be moral inheritor of the Black Prince and true bearer of England's royalty. Only at the end of the play does his son's alienation give a hint of the nemesis that threatens him. He complains of the wastrel Prince of Wales just before facing York's rebellious son. Bolingbroke seems unconscious of any parallel, but the suggestion is that disorder in the state growing out of his usurpation has put an unnatural strain on the bonds of father and son. The isolation characteristic of Shakespeare's kings, and especially of his usurpers, has enveloped the new ruler. At the end of the play, the only member of his family who appears with him in unshaken loyalty is his ineffectual old uncle York. Tainted with his cousin's blood, Bolingbroke suffers from a guilt and loneliness that run deeper than pragmatic politics.

It is in Richard, however, that Shakespeare first develops with full power the tragic effects of isolation. Richard III freely chooses to alienate himself from his family, and the early Richard II does much the same thing. His counselors are not his wise uncles, but the favorites Bushy, Bagot, and Greene. He has had one uncle killed and confiscates the estate of another. His flippant cynicism with his coterie about his kinsmen Bolingbroke and Gaunt (I.iv) is less evil than Richard III's ironic scorn at family bonds only because Richard II is weaker. He is an amateur playing at professional villainy. In the scene (II.i) that most clearly establishes his guilt, both Gaunt and York suggest that he has repudiated his heroic father's example. The cavalier way in which he names his uncle York to govern in his absence suggests, not only his folly in appointing a weak man, but also his bland confidence in an affectionate loyalty that he has just come near to shattering. He exploits the family bond that he is not willing to support himself.

But if this Richard willfully chooses his isolation, the later Richard feels the weight of loneliness. Stripped of the realities of power and of any meaningful personal contact, he tries to generate these things verbally.[10] Over and over again he creates ceremonies to replace the lost ceremonial pomp of his office.

Because he knows that he has lost the reality of power, the ceremonies are aimless and perverse. Since the ideals of succession and kingly right that he appeals to are real ones, his voice every now and then catches a note of prophetic insight, but it soon dwindles into petulance and self-pity.

This new Richard appears at the midpoint of the play, after his absence in Ireland. The sight of a king weeping and caressing the earth establishes the perversity of his sorrow:

> As a long-parted mother with her child
> Plays fondly with her tears and smiles in meeting,
> So weeping, smiling, greet I thee, my earth,
> And do thee favours with my royal hands.
>
> (III.ii.8-11)

He inverts the normal figure of the earth as mother, a figure that Bolingbroke uses of English soil at I.iii.306-7. The effeminacy of his language is the first sign of how weak Richard is when he can no longer depend on his royal power.[11] Lest this scene be taken for a stylized representation of normal grief, Shakespeare provides certain guides for the audience, including an earlier episode of just such conventional grief. After Richard sails for Ireland, his queen Isabel has premonitions of disaster. She expresses her fears and Bushy consoles her in the most conceit-filled euphuistic style (II.ii.1-40). But Richard is alone in the extravagant language of his landing and conscious of his followers' embarrassed disapproval: "Mock not my senseless conjuration, lords" (III.ii.23). Also his style fluctuates with his mood, so that no established pattern of conventional grief can be felt. The artificial method is internalized in one character and thus made an expression of his detachment from reality. In Isabel and Richard, Shakespeare contrasts an artificial character and a character who willfully pursues artificiality.

Having forfeited his place in the state and in his own family, Richard can only play with the remnants of his glory. When he confronts Bolingbroke at Flint Castle, his first speech is an impressive declaration of divine right, ending in a prophecy that foresees the whole course of the Wars of the Roses:

> But ere the crown he looks for live in peace,
> Ten thousand bloody crowns of mothers' sons
> Shall ill become the flower of England's face,
> Change the complexion of her maid-pale peace
> To scarlet indignation and bedew
> Her pastures' grass with faithful English blood.
> (III.iii.95-100)

Here in passing is the familiar use of a general family reference in order to intensify a broad view of disaster. Even the cold-blooded Northumberland seems taken aback by this speech, but he is soon moved to scorn as Richard's voice rises to hysteria. By the time that the waning king descends to the base court, self-consciously pointing out the symbolism of the act, his language has become shrill and maudlin. His next appeal to the family is the petulant irony of calling Bolingbroke his heir. In the deposition scene he turns the renunciation of his inherited crown into a loss even

of "that name was given me at the font" (IV.i.256).
(The speech is more naturally read as the embroidery
of Richard's despair than as an obscure reference to
the legend of his bastardy recounted by Froissart.) To
break the unity of the king's two bodies, his office and
his private self, is to destroy his personal identity, which
is as much based on inheritance as his crown.[12]

One might have expected Shakespeare to make considerable use of the queen, whose continued loyalty to
her husband counterpoints the nobles' treachery, but
he does not. Only once does Richard talk to her on
stage, when she intercepts him on the way to the
Tower. The result is a conventionally lyric expression
of joint sorrow, given a touch of irony by the presence
of the cynical Northumberland through most of it.
Again Richard is more self-consciously dramatic than
Isabel as he arranges (and characteristically changes
his mind about) an "inverted ceremony":[13]

> Doubly divorc'd! Bad men, you violate
> A two-fold marriage—'twixt my crown and me,
> And then betwixt me and my married wife.
> Let me unkiss the oath 'twixt thee and me;
> And yet not so, for with a kiss 'twas made.
> Part us, Northumberland.
>
> (V.i.71-76)

The figure of marriage to the crown is not quite conventional and so loses the power of orthodox commonplace, and it lacks the startling inevitability of Shakespeare's richer metaphors. Later Richard uses Constance's image of loving and marrying a personified

sorrow (93-94), with perhaps the same suggestion of passionate excessiveness. For the most part, however, neither the characterization nor the emotion gets beyond conventional (and not very interesting) dramatic technique.

To Richard the family is little more than a useful figure of speech. Having forfeited the loyalty of his own kin, he can find little consolation in his wife's love. In his prison cell he makes only one reference to the family, a strained conceit that describes the working of his imagination (V.v.6-10).[14] Even this late he shows only the most general consciousness of his guilt and none at all of his crimes against the right of succession, on which he bases his own sense of injustice. Alone, self-destroyed, even now self-deceived, he achieves only the lesser triumph of fighting bravely against his assassins. In his world nothing is real enough to make his isolation from the ties of family love tragically painful. Paradoxically enough, his hard-headed -rival Bolingbroke will turn out to be vulnerable to that kind of suffering.

The characteristic device of *Richard II*, what sets it off most clearly from the earlier histories, is its use of artificial poetic and dramatic modes to establish different levels of reality. There is something to Tillyard's distinction between the ceremonial old order and the practical world of the New Men,[15] but more important is the distinction between the ideal and the real. Artificial rhetoric can suggest hypocrisy, as it does in the first scene, or a genuine ideal with prophetic force, as in Carlisle's and Richard's warnings for the future. Or it can suggest self-deceived unreality, Richard's characteristic state after his return from Ireland. Shakespeare's audience was alert to shifts in dramatic technique and tolerant of the most startling juxtapositions of realistic and conventional elements. They were accustomed to see the family as an emblem of disorder in the state, and they must have noticed this device in *Richard II*. All the familiar pattern of violated order and inherited guilt is sketched out there. Richard's crime against his uncles begins the cycle, and Bolingbroke's crime against his king and cousin extends it.

Nevertheless, this technique is less obtrusive in *Richard II* than in the first tetralogy once the ceremonial use in the early scenes fades away. Shakespeare is now more interested in another subject, the psychology of kingship. He shows, not only the qualities that make Richard lose his crown, but also what happens to his vision of himself when he is deprived of the position that gives him identity. Richard imaginatively projects himself into a simpler world where right and power are the same, though in flashes he is bitterly conscious of the self-deception. But for him there is no bearable alternative. Because he lives in an unreal world, he cannot have a truly intimate relationship. That is why the parting between him and Isabel has to be conventional. Though his suffering is real enough, it is almost entirely egocentric.

Consequently the family in *Richard II* hangs in a kind of limbo. As an emblem for political morality, it suffers the fate of all ideals in this play. The moral voice of Richard's wise uncle, John of Gaunt, is real enough, but Gaunt dies. Transferred to Richard's emotional tirades, the old code becomes illusory, unsupported by real physical power. On the other hand, Shakespeare cannot explore family bonds in a more psychological way because of his tragic hero's special character. The great dramatic power of *Richard II* lies in its study of a ruler whose weakness betrays him as a king and isolates him as a man; of course, the fact that it does not further explore the dramatic potentialities of the family detracts in no way from that value. Also its technical development beyond the first tetralogy, its subtle probing into the psyche of a man, opens the way for just such an exploration in the Henry IV plays.

Conclusion: *The Two Experimental Plays*

In a sense all of Shakespeare's plays are experiments. He never simply repeats an earlier success, his own or another's. Nevertheless, *King John* and *Richard II* are more precisely experimental plays. At least in part they abandon the dramatic structure that Shakespeare worked out in the Henry VI plays and demonstrated complete in *Richard III*. The theme of political disorder having led him to study the bad king, perhaps he found the figure of Richard III too theatrical, too much a hypothetical construction like the Senecan tyrant and the Vice, too little a recognizable human being. Or perhaps he merely wanted to avoid repeating himself. At any rate, John and Richard, though bad kings, are remarkably different from the heroic villain Richard III. Not only are they weaker men, but they resist, and suffer from, the isolation that he relishes.

John clings first to his mother and then to Faulconbridge, and Richard laments even his horse's disloyalty. Incapacity to feel personal bonds is a perverted kind of strength to Richard Crookback, but in
these two kings it is part of their weakness. Neither has
self-knowledge enough to realize that part of his crime
is against the bonds of family, and so both seek an
affection that they have forfeited.

Because of their weakness, John and Richard II do
not dominate their plays completely. The vigorous
Faulconbridge steals much of the interest from John,
and Bolingbroke fails to do so from Richard only
through a *tour de force* of dramatic shading and high-
lighting. Shakespeare's explorations carry him beyond
any severe decorum of style or form. As a result *King
John* is a hodgepodge of brilliant fragments and work-
manlike joints, and even *Richard II* is not entirely
focused either as a psychological portrait or as a political study.

On the whole the family continues its previous role
in these two experimental plays, though the political
ideas that it echoes no longer seem primary in their
dramatic life. But even as this symbolic function wanes
in significance, one kind of family relationship receives
special attention: inheritance, the handing-on of power
and an ethical and political code from father to son.
In imagery, in short episodes, and in character portrayal, fathers and sons occupy an important place
while marriage fades in importance. It is as though
Shakespeare were reaching toward a new potentiality
in the family as a dramatic subject, one that will find
triumphant expression in the Henry IV plays.

RICHARD II

[1] *Shakespeare's History Plays* (London, 1944), pp. 244-52.

[2] Cf. the discussion of blood in Richard D. Altick, "Symphonic Imagery in *Richard II*," *PMLA* 62 (1957), 345-47.

[3] Cf. the excellent discussion of family honor in Michael Quinn, " 'The King Is Not Himself': The Personal Tragedy of Richard II," *Studies in Philology* 56 (1959), 174-78. James Winny, *The Player King: A Theme of Shakespeare's Histories* (New York, 1968), pp. 73-85, discusses father-and-son imagery in the play.

[4] Shakespeare seems to assume that his audience knows these earlier events. His company may have been performing *Woodstock,* an anonymous chronicle play on the earlier part of Richard's reign, if indeed *Woodstock* predates *Richard II.* On the other hand, he may be relying on knowledge from *A Mirror for Magistrates* and other, perhaps untraceable, sources.

[5] One other father and son, Northumberland and Hotspur, appear in *Richard II.* Northumberland plays a role of some importance, but little is made of his relationship with his son. Still, the contrast of their characters foreshadows the use to be made of them in *Henry IV.* Hotspur's bluntness to the rising Bolingbroke contrasts with his father's oily flattery. Just after Northumberland pointedly omits Richard's title and is reproved for it by York, Hotspur enters and speaks in quite a different vein (III.iii.20-26).

[6] Hence there is symbolic weight in Bolingbroke's charge that Bushy and Greene have

> Rac'd out my imprese, leaving me no sign,
> Save men's opinions and my living blood,
> To show the world I am a gentleman. (III.i.25-27)

[7] "Dramatic Techniques and Interpretation in 'Richard II'," *Early Shakespeare,* ed. John Russell Brown and Bernard Harris, Stratford-upon-Avon Studies, No. 3 (London, 1961), p. 465. Robert Adger Law, "Deviations from Holinshed in *Richard II*," University of Texas *Studies in English* 29 (1950), 95, points out that according to Holinshed the Duchess of York was Aumerle's stepmother. Presumably Shakespeare ignores this fact in order to make the family conflict more straightforward.

[8] "Never, in an age of drama marked by discursive self-revelation, has a character disclosed his traits with such economy and understatement" (Brents Stirling, "Bolingbroke's Decision," *Shakespeare Quarterly* 2 [1951], 34). This article is perhaps the best single analysis of his motivation.

[9] Irving Ribner, "Bolingbroke, a True Machiavellian," *Modern Language Quarterly* 9 (1948), 177-84, argues that Bolingbroke is a true Machiavellian as opposed to the Elizabethan stage distortion, but

his argument is qualified by the fact that most of the parallels with Machiavelli's doctrines are already implicit in Holinshed's narrative. Shakespeare is imitating nature, not *The Prince*.

[10] Peter Ure, *King Richard II*, New Arden Shakespeare, 5th ed. (Cambridge, Mass., 1961), pp. lxviii-lxxii, vigorously objects to descriptions of Richard as self-consciously verbal, a poet rather than a king. He is properly reacting against critical excesses, but surely it is fair to say that Richard is conscious of his own language in a way that Othello or Macbeth (or John of Gaunt) is not. Using verse is of course a dramatic convention, but as always Shakespeare is perfectly capable of turning the convention into a point of characterization.

[11] In "Phaethon: The Metaphysical Tension between the Ego and the Universe in English Poetry," *Accent* 16 (1956), 30, Parker Tyler argues that the figure also shows Richard pursuing "the illusion of divine parenthood." But even in this expression of *hybris* his effeminate weakness is clear.

[12] See the valuable study of *Richard II* in Ernst H. Kantorowicz, *The King's Two Bodies: A Study in Mediaeval Political Theology* (Princeton, N.J., 1957).

[13] The term is from Walter Pater, "Shakespeare's English Kings," *Appreciations, With an Essay on Style*, Vol. V of *The Works of Walter Pater* (New York, 1901), 198.

[14] Quinn relates Richard's failure to have an heir to this passage. "In his last hour he is reduced to making his brain and soul parody the sex-act, so as to breed, instead of children, 'A generation of still-breeding thoughts'" ("'The King Is Not Himself,'" p. 183).

[15] Tillyard, pp. 244-63. Peter G. Phialas, "The Medieval in *Richard II*," *Shakespeare Quarterly* 12 (1961), 305-10, emphasizes the contrast between the time of the Black Prince and Richard's degenerate medieval reign. The article is a valuable supplement to Tillyard's view, but the two are more compatible than Phialas suggests. For a recent development of Tillyard's contrast, applied to the whole second tetralogy, see Alvin Kernan, "The Henriad: Shakespeare's Major History Plays," *Yale Review* 69 (1969), 3-32.

Chapter VI

THE HENRY IV PLAYS

S HAKESPEARE'S Henry IV plays explore the theme of political order with a new depth and subtlety.[1] Not only does the state pass through civil war to harmony, but Prince Hal develops into a king fit to lead his newly united state in war against France. Although political order is central to the plays, Shakespeare uses a more personal order, that of the family, to illuminate his theme. In the early history plays harmony and strife in family relationships become symbols of order and disorder in the kingdom. This device expresses political ideas by analogy with another realm of experience. But in the two Henry IV plays the symbol merges with its referent; Shakespeare displays the quest for political order as fundamentally like the quest for personal order within the family. The values are the same, the problems the same; only the scale is different.

In Hal and his father the historical given of Shakespeare's plot combines the two levels: prince and king, son and father. While Henry IV struggles to keep his throne and the rebels to replace him, England is hungry for renewed order. Though he is in many ways a good ruler, he cannot be the hero-king who compels loyalty as well as submission. Prince Hal is to be such a king, but before he can assume his destined role, he must attain personal maturity. He must find a viable order for his own life, one centered on his duty to become England's king. Only thus will he be saved from self-destruction or personal insignificance, and only thus will England be saved (for a time) from civil war.

Finding in his sources the legend of Hal the wild prince, Shakespeare turns it into an expression of this theme. Like any young man reaching maturity, Hal must emulate his father's role, but at the same time he must escape his father in order to establish his autonomy. Even in the ideal family this task is difficult. In *1 Henry VI* young Talbot must defy his father's command to flee the battlefield so that he may be like his father and hence show a family loyalty deeper than explicit obedience. But Hal's father is a guilty man, one whose piety is tainted by Richard II's blood on his hands. In his personal inheritance from his father, Hal faces the same problem as the realm, how to generate an ordered future out of a disordered present. He must transcend his inheritance without denying it. It is part of the extraordinary scope of the Henry IV plays to study this spiritual process. An abstractly conceived Providence can bring peace to the England of *Richard III* because the process is external to Richard, but only a newly personal and psychological drama can show Hal's development into the king who will lead England to unity and glory.

The portrayal of Hal's growth follows a popular

motif in Elizabethan drama, the Prodigal Son story.[2] Hal leaves his responsibilities and his father for a life of tavern brawls, behavior typical of the prodigal, though Hal avoids contamination with the worst evils around him, reckless gambling, wenching, and such. Falstaff, "that villainous abominable misleader of youth" (II.iv.456), parallels a Vice-figure like Cacurgus in *Misogonus*. Henry IV has much in common with the typical father, noble and sententious but somewhat ineffectual toward his son. The virtuous elder brother of the parable turns up in *Misogonus* as a long-lost heir; there may be a hint of this motif in the contrast between Hal and Prince John as well as in Henry IV's wish that Hotspur, Hal's rival, were his son. Appropriately enough, the parable of the Prodigal Son occurs among Falstaff's frequent allusions to scripture.[3] This theme extends through both plays, since Hal is not completely reconciled to his father until the end of *2 Henry IV*.

In one sense Shakespeare is burlesquing an old dramatic form as John Marston does in *Histrio-Mastix*. After all, it is the prodigal who mischievously denounces his tempter as "that reverend vice, that grey iniquity, that father ruffian, that vanity in years" (*1 Henry IV*, II.iv.447-49). And Falstaff himself delights in acting the prodigal, corrupted by his evil companions: "Before I knew thee, Hal, I knew nothing, and now am I, if a man should speak truly, little better than one of the wicked" (*1 Henry IV*, I.ii.90-92). This lightheartedness suggests even more clearly than Hal's soliloquy at the end of I.ii that he will not be significantly corrupted. Yet at the same time Falstaff is a serious threat to Hal's maturity, and the reconciliation with his father is a necessary step in his growth.

Thus Shakespeare exploits the human validity of the pattern even while smiling at its dramatic absurdities. There is a perilous solemnity in the moralizing of a form that adapts Plautine and Terentian comedy to Renaissance ethical education, and Shakespeare punctures that solemnity. At the same time, the dramatized parable offers a pattern for using the wild-prince legends. For all Shakespeare's modifications to burlesque the pattern and to make it psychologically plausible, he uses the religious theme embodied in it. In the parable the Prodigal Son restored to his father is man restored to God, and in the Elizabethan system of correspondences the king is to his kingdom as God is to the universe. Hal's reconciliation with his father symbolizes a larger commitment to all that is good and orderly in the world.

1 Henry IV

The first of the two plays has an obvious division into two levels, the public story of the rebellion of the Percies and the private story of Hal's dissipations with Falstaff. Part of what raises this play above the typical Elizabethan two-plot drama is the ingenuity with which the two are interwoven, so that the Falstaff scenes parody many of the episodes and characters of the serious scenes. However, there is a third plot, less extended than the other two, that helps to mediate between them. It is the story of Hal's estrangement from his father and their reconciliation. Only in this plot is Hal clearly the central figure, though all three contribute to the most important theme of this and the next play, Hal's preparation for kingship over a united England. The rebellion of the Percies provides the battlefield on which he can prove his chivalric merit; and Hotspur, the dominant figure of the Percy camp, gives a dramatic contrast that illuminates Hal's growth. The scenes with Falstaff show Hal avoiding his duty, but they also help to educate him in the whole order (and disorder) of his future kingdom. Although Shakespeare allows us to glimpse the domestic life of the Percies, they live primarily in a public world, a world of treaties and defiances and battles, of blank verse. Although Falstaff appears, ludicrously out of place, at Shrewsbury, his is essentially a private world without clocks, a world of sack and tavern jests and highway robbery, of prose.

What gives the relationship of Henry IV and Hal special complexity is that in it the public and private worlds merge. As king and prince they embody all the political ideas implied in that relationship throughout the history plays. Hal must inherit the heroic and regal virtues of his father so that he may be a king worthy of his Lancastrian forebears. To teach Hal this lesson, Henry points to the ominous example of Richard II, who betrayed the heritage of the Black Prince with a frivolity that Henry sees in Hal too. Also the public theme of inherited guilt is an important one. Henry fears that his crime in deposing Richard will infect the kingdom even after his death (and Hal in *Henry V* shares that fear). As a public figure Henry IV has a double significance. He is the king, the center of order and virtue in the realm and hence the prime object of Hal's duty. But at the same time he is guilty; all the conscious piety of his life cannot entirely justify him, even to himself.

If Henry were simply a public figure, an emblem like John of Gaunt in *Richard II,* this ambiguity of meaning would destroy him as a dramatic character. What saves him is that he is given a private identity, an individual nature that expresses itself apart from his public stance. A public symbol cannot be ambiguous, but a man can be so various as to evoke two different symbolisms. In the same way Hal can both laugh at and be the Prodigal Son because he has a private identity that transcends both burlesque and symbolism. Henry IV and Hal are not only king and prince; they are also a very concrete father and son, going through all the painful misunderstanding that fathers and sons have always faced.

Henry appears first of all as king. As John Dover Wilson points out,[4] he speaks for himself and the kingdom in his opening words:

> So shaken as we are, so wan with care,
> Find we a time for frighted peace to pant,
> And breathe short-winded accents of new broils
> To be commenc'd in stronds afar remote:
> No more the thirsty entrance of this soil
> Shall daub her lips with her own children's blood.
>
> (I.i.1-6)

The sense of powers declining under strain, the desperate longing for peace, and the vague hope for glory in foreign wars—all these Henry shares with his land. It is a sign of his worthiness as a king that he expresses so accurately the spirit of his realm. The stark family image of lines 5-6, with its biblical echo,[5] is typical of the severe formality of the speech. Henry's language shows the tightly linked world of Elizabethan correspondences, in which the state is a family and civil war opposes those "of one substance bred," so that they war "Against acquaintance, kindred, and allies" (11, 16).

Since most of the audience must have known that this was to be a play about civil war, they would notice the self-deception in Henry's prediction of peace; and it soon emerges that he is willfully deceiving himself, because he knows that England is still wracked with strife and even that the Percies show ominous signs of disloyalty. Henry represents a generation of Englishmen who have fought each other and will go on fighting until they can hardly remember the purpose of the battles and can only say:

> We are all diseas'd,
> And with our surfeiting, and wanton hours,
> Have brought ourselves into a burning fever,
> And we must bleed for it.
> (*2 Henry IV*, IV.i.54-57)

After his description of civil war in terms of violence within the family, there is irony in Henry's turning to speak with pain of his son's degeneracy. At the moment he seems unconscious of any connection between public and familial disorder. It may seem like a heartless repudiation of family bonds when he wishes:

> O that it could be prov'd
> That some night-tripping fairy had exchang'd
> In cradle-clothes our children where they lay,
> And call'd mine Percy, his Plantagenet!
>
> (85-88)

But the suffering is clear enough behind the petulant rejection. It is "my young Harry" (85) whose dishonor he feels; the repeated "mine" of the passage shows the grief of an estranged father, not unfeeling repudiation. If the audience perceived the irony of his wish to go to the Holy Land, they must also have seen the happier irony of his despair at the character of the future hero-king, the legendary example of wildness reformed. This speech establishes a contrast between the two young men that runs through the play and reaches its climax in their confrontation at Shrewsbury.

If in the first scene Henry IV seems like an old man, tired and sick from the strains of rule, it soon becomes apparent that he has not lost the strength of will and imposing presence that won him the crown. He sends for the Percies to explain their holding back the Scottish prisoners, and when Worcester shows signs of more pride than is fitting in a subject, Henry abruptly banishes him from the court. Questionable though his accession is, he is a royal king, and Hal can learn only from him the dignity that a king must have. The curious episode of the men in Henry's coats whom Douglas slays at Shrewsbury raises the issue of who is really king[6] when Douglas challenges Henry:

> What art thou
> That counterfeit'st the person of a king?
>
> (V.iv.26-27)

But Douglas himself gives a worthy answer:

> I fear thou art another counterfeit,
> And yet, in faith, thou bearest thee like a king.
>
> (34-35)

By a great act of will Henry is able to bear himself like a king. If the effort gradually saps his strength, there is little external evidence of his decline until his sickness in *2 Henry IV*. Only in one scene of this play does he fully reveal the private man behind the king, when he is alone with his son in III.ii. The sense of tension, of a will kept forcibly taut in his public appearances, suggests the terrible penalty of being king.

In contrast with his father in the opening scene, Hal in the second appears young, full of vitality, and gaily irresponsible. While his father wrestles with the problems of state, Falstaff and Hal can jest about how he will behave as king. "I prithee sweet wag, when thou art king, as God save thy Grace—Majesty I should say, for grace thou wilt have none" (I.ii.16-18). The fact that the major theme of Hal's development toward the ideal king can be suggested in a pun shows the characteristic tone of the scene. When he comes to this world where time is irrelevant and chivalry no more than the code of the highwayman, he is escaping from the court, from his father, and from his own place as heir apparent.

One can take too solemnly his assertion of virtue in the much-discussed soliloquy that closes the scene. The speech may seem priggish, as though Hal were condescending to sport with Falstaff even while maintaining a severe inner virtue. He says, "I know you all" (I.ii.190), implying that Falstaff's sinfulness is no threat to his self-confident virtue. However, direct exposition of one's moral state is characteristic of Elizabethan soliloquies. It is dangerous to read too much self-consciousness into Hal's proclamation of his own worth. Many critics note that this soliloquy is primarily a device to assure the audience of Hal's final reformation, an assurance especially needed just after he has agreed to join in a highway robbery. And his treatment of Falstaff is not really condescending; he too obviously rejoices in the battle of wits that keeps them on equal terms.

On the other hand, the fact that the soliloquy is a conventional device need not compel one to take it as absolutely true. Only someone determined to believe in Hal's spotless virtue (or his priggishness) could accept at face value the argument that a king gains his people's loyalty from having been a youthful sinner. No doubt Hal plans to reform, but he has not undertaken his sins in order to abandon them with a spectacular public gesture. There is an undertone to his argument that suggests his main reason for avoiding the court:

If all the year were playing holidays,
To sport would be as tedious as to work;
But when they seldom come, they wish'd-for come,
And nothing pleaseth but rare accidents.

(199-202)

Explicitly he is arguing that the contrast between a dissolute youth and a reformed king heightens the latter, just as the contrast with working days makes holidays pleasant. Yet at the same time he half-admits to snatching a few last bits of pleasure before assuming the heavy duties of kingship. Just right is Dr. Johnson's description of the soliloquy as "a natural picture of a great mind offering excuses to itself and palliating those follies which it can neither justify nor forsake."[7]

Hal's sport with Falstaff is not only a young man's escape from responsibility, however. The public world of the play is one of disorder and treachery. Hotspur is caught in the political schemes of his father and uncle and manipulated by them. Henry IV is a nobler man than his former allies (except for Hotspur), but even he is trapped by his dubious past into suspicion and cold scheming. His projected crusade to the Holy Land is never more than a dream of expiation. Thus Hal escapes a tainted atmosphere by leaving the court. The evils of the tavern to which he turns are "like their father that begets them, gross as a mountain, open, palpable" (II.iv.220-21). Even though Falstaff's company sometimes parodies the public world, it is not corrupted by the pervasive disorder of the kingdom. "A plague upon it when thieves cannot be true one to another!" (II.ii.27-28). Falstaff's complaint foreshadows the disintegration among the rebels, but in fact the disloyalty in his band of "thieves" is harmless and even illusory.

In general the vices of Falstaff's group are timeless; the characters themselves are an anachronism brought into the play from Elizabethan life. This habit is not unusual among low-comedy scenes in Tudor drama, but here it is significant in that it provides an escape from the political disorder of the public scenes. In the three parts of *Henry VI* disorder spreads out from the court to infect the whole kingdom, but in *1 Henry IV* the life of England goes on in spite of treachery and rebellion among the governors. Hostlers worry about the price of oats, and Falstaff about the purity of sack. Leaving the court, Hal finds England with all its vices and jests, but also its abiding strength. What Faulconbridge brings to the court of King John, Hal reaches by going out into London.

Yet if Hal can gain strength from contact with English life, there is also the threat of forgetting his special role as England's future king. Just as he must escape from the court and his father to grow beyond them, so he must escape the unreasonable claims on him of his London companions. "O for a fine thief of the age of two and twenty or thereabouts: I am heinously unprovided," says Falstaff (III.iii.187-89). He is unprovided because Hal has kept himself a king's son on a lark. His characteristic defense against Falstaff is his irony, an amused detachment from whatever he is doing. Curiously enough, it is the same quality that allows him to show no concern for the deed when he proves his chivalric merit by killing Hotspur, the key symbolic act of the play. His nature is not "subdued / To what it works in" (Sonnet 111), whether he rubs elbows with Falstaff or fights against Hotspur.

Critics find this ironic detachment offensive in Hal, not when it shows itself as *sprezzatura,* the nonchalance of Castiglione's courtier,[8] but when it rebuffs Falstaff's claims to intimacy. There is unconscious humor in the fugitive and cloistered vice of literary scholars who condemn Hal for repudiating the free life of a tavern roisterer and highway robber; one explanation of such a view is the absence in our day of much feeling for the importance of calling. Hal is called to be the next king of England, and so he cannot be an ordinary man. He is not denying his humanity in accepting his duty to prepare for royalty,[9] because a man's vocation is the center of his manhood. In this play his calling is defined by his rivalry with Hotspur. He must demonstrate to his father and all the land that he is the true prince, not only in title but in worth. Thus he can turn from the boyish jest of giving Falstaff a company of foot soldiers to a vigorous assertion of his family's destiny:

> The land is burning, Percy stands on high,
> And either we or they must lower lie.
> (III.iii.202-3)

Henry IV and his son come together for the first time at III.ii. Ironically, Shakespeare has just shown the charming domesticity of the rebel camp when he turns to the estrangement of the king and crown prince. Henry's speeches to his son are curiously poised between his typical stiff formality and a father's anxious sincerity. His opening words are full of the traditional doctrines of the family. Thus for the first time he acknowledges that Hal's wildness may be punishment for "my mistreadings" (11). He measures Hal against the ideal of aristocratic inheritance, asking how he can reconcile "the greatness of thy blood" (16) with such low pursuits. He misunderstands his son, since he assumes that Hal is "match'd withal, and grafted to" these pleasures (15), the imagery suggesting that their corruption has entered the fibers of his being. But this speech is so formal that it suggests only abstract parenthood, and Hal's reply is in the same vein. They have expressed their abstract relationship, but little of the personal feeling in it.

Up to this point Henry has hidden the intensity of his emotions behind a mask of formality, but in his next speech his grief precariously warps the formality. After an affectionate "Harry" in line 29, he quickly pulls back into the commonplaces of aristocratic inheritance. He again charges Hal with betraying the tradition of his ancestors and losing the affection of his kinsmen. The king's hurt ego swings around to brood on his own past successes as he compares Hal with Richard II. He asserts that Hal has repudiated the moral heritage of the Lancastrians for Richard's corrupted "line" (85). (Primarily the word means "category" here, but it suggests the whole idea of a station in life established by birth.) His emotion gradually rises during the speech until he suddenly finds himself weeping as he complains of his son's neglect in what is no longer a king's reproof but the complaint of a lonely father.

Hal's reply to this display of emotion is embarrassed and terse, though it may reveal a deeper contrition than did his first speech. But the tide of Henry's grief cannot stop, and so he returns to comparing Hal with Richard. Now he raises the most irritating comparison, that with Hotspur. He contrasts Hal's dynastic inheritance with Hotspur's supposed moral superiority:

> Now by my sceptre, and my soul to boot,
> He hath more worthy interest to the state
> Than thou the shadow of succession.
>
> (97-99)

This pragmatic king has learned that even a title as unstained as Richard II's is only a shadow without *virtù*, the quality that he thinks he sees in Hotspur. The way that he associates Hotspur with himself hints that he wishes Hotspur were his heir. But that wish is no more than a desperate evasion of his parental grief, as the petulance of his next few lines indicates. He even charges that Hal will fight under Percy against his own family.

This final turn allows Hal to feel a cleansing anger. His characteristic irony overcome by hurt love and pride, he makes his most complete and open declaration of aims. The abrupt, almost non-metrical beginning suggests his anger: "Do not think so, you shall not find it so" (129). And the next few lines illuminate its cause; if Hotspur is the barrier between Hal and Henry's love, then Hotspur must die. By Henry's own standard the warrior ideal is the measure of moral worth, and Hal means to establish himself before his father and the kingdom. Already the duel of Act V is foreshadowed and weighted with public and private meaning. Conquering Hotspur will cleanse Hal's name and make him a hero worthy of royalty, but at the same time it will complete the reconciliation of this father and son. Hence the angry reproach of Hal's contrast between "This gallant Hotspur, this all-praised knight, / And your unthought-of Harry" (140-41).

Like most fathers Henry is only too eager to be reconciled. Delighted by his son's heroic zeal and by the affection implied in Hal's hurt feelings, he regains his kingly dignity and his confidence together:

> A hundred thousand rebels die in this—
> Thou shalt have charge and sovereign trust herein.
> (160-61)

Now that he knows the cleavage in his own house to be healed, he can face the challenge of the Percy rebellion with poise.[10] When Blunt reports the gathering of the enemy, Henry gives orders with brisk efficiency and assigns Hal an important place in the plans. This father and son standing together are a symbol of unity in the realm, just as in *1 Henry VI* Talbot and his son fighting together stand for the unity that will die with them. But because Shakespeare has shown their reconciliation in an intensely personal scene, Henry and Hal are more than just symbols of order. Above all, the scene is a step in Hal's growth toward full readiness for kingship, but it also reveals

Henry's human struggle to endure the weight of kingly office. The symbol of unity is there, but it is surrounded by a richness of meanings such as the early Shakespeare never achieved.

The king and Hal appear together again at Shrewsbury, now in perfect harmony. Henry is so full of confidence that he can laugh at the ill omen of a gloomy morning. Throughout the day Hal is the picture of a true prince, extorting praise even from his enemies. With becoming humility in his words, he challenges Hotspur to single combat.[11] Henry forbids that, perhaps because of still-continuing doubts in his son, but mainly because it would be foolish to give up the advantage of superior numbers. In the battle Hal shows brotherly pride at Prince John's valor, and afterward he allows his brother the honor of giving Douglas his freedom. When Hal saves his father's life from Douglas, the king recalls the charges that Hal has sought his death. The sincerity of Hal's indignation is supported by his deeds, and in fact only the king's remark makes him point out the significance of his act. Finally Hotspur, Hal's rival, dies under his sword, and the last picture of the prince is with his family on the battlefield won by their united valor. If the expression of this newly firm tie between the king and his son is almost entirely public and formal at Shrewsbury, those qualities make the last scenes complementary to the personal reconciliation of III.ii. Shrewsbury establishes the forces of order as dominant in the kingdom, and its final moment is this public symbol of unity, a king and his crown prince, reconciled and victorious.

The path of Hal's growth is a great arc. He must

move away from his father and the court so that he may find his personal autonomy. He must revitalize the Lancastrian line by renewed contact with the source of all political power, the commonwealth itself. Yet there is peril in this journey. If he plunges too deeply into the world of Falstaff and his companions, he will lose contact with his own heritage, with the birth that calls him to prepare himself for England's throne. And so the arc turns back. Hal must return to his father and prove his worthiness to be the Lancastrian heir. Now he must act for himself, yet to defend the primacy of the House of Lancaster. Only half-understanding what has happened to his son, Henry IV senses the ardor and enthusiasm that Hal has brought with him. The returned prodigal is the new hope of the forces of order, and especially of the king his father. "For this my son was dead, and is alive again: he was lost and is found." Hal, and with him the Lancastrian line, are renewed.

The Percies and the Lancastrians.—The middle plot of *1 Henry IV* is, then, a subtle and complex version of the ancient story of the Prodigal Son. Both of the other two plots are so arranged as to comment on this theme of father and son. Most obvious is the parallel between Hotspur and Hal. From Worcester's first haughty reference to "our house" (I.iii.10) through the final combat between the two young representatives of the two houses, the Percies are contrasted with the Lancasters. As the Duke of York's family in the Henry VI plays draws together to defend his claim to the throne, so the Percies set forth their in-law as rightful king. Like the Yorks this group bound together by kinship and wedlock seems a solid unity at first, but weaknesses begin to appear. Among the signs of internal disorder is the bickering in III.i over a kingdom that, it now appears, is not to be given to its rightful king entire but to be divided into three parts among the conspirators. Hotspur's amusingly petty quarrels with Glendower only partly obscure the horror of his proposal. The conspirators manage to paper over their differences and call in the ladies to an ironically charming scene of marital affection. It is possible that there is a hint of symbolic disorder in Mortimer's inability to talk to his Welsh-speaking wife, but the emphasis of the scene is on a domestic happiness that the plotters are leaving to take arms against their king. Once again there is a glimpse of the normal life against which this play shows the Percy rebellion.

As in the House of Lancaster, so there is a contrast between the generations of the Percies. Worcester and Northumberland illustrate Machiavellian policy gone to seed. They make some show of political scheming, but in fact they proceed spitefully out of a mixture of offended pride and thwarted ambition. They manipulate Hotspur to gain his support in I.iii, but by sheer youthful vigor he promptly wrests control of the rebel movement from them. When they bend to his superiority in virtue, the consequence is that the conspiracy is at the mercy of his impetuosity. He reveals the plot to a man who even he admits is likely to reveal it to the king "in very sincerity of fear and cold heart" (II.iii.30-31). He goes out of his way to antagonize Glendower, their sensitive Welsh ally, and

it may not be coincidental that Glendower fails them
at Shrewsbury. The night before the battle Hotspur
rashly favors an immediate attack on the king's forces,
an ill-conceived plan if, as seems likely, we are to
accept the objections of the sensible and attractive
Vernon. But Hotspur is growing in responsibility even
then. As the bad news of a mighty enemy and the
failure of his own reserves mounts up, he prepares with
a new sobriety to go forth to what he must know is
almost certain defeat.

His father's failure to support the rebellion does
most to doom their cause, as Hotspur at first acknowledges. Worcester expresses the point of Northumberland's absence:

> The quality and hair of our attempt
> Brooks no division.
>
> (IV.i.61-62)

Rebels, the proponents of disorder, can succeed only
through their internal unity, as Falstaff implies of
thieves. The central unit of this plot is the House of
the Percies, and so when a break divides that unit,
the rebellion is doomed.

Just after Worcester's comment Hotspur hears that
the Prince of Wales, whom he thought estranged from
his father and lost in dissipation, is present and acting
the part of a chivalric hero. Thus he learns that the
division in his rival's family is healed. Again his own
family shows bad faith within itself when his uncle
Worcester fails to tell him of the king's offered clem-
ency. Worcester deceives his nephew out of a prudent

fear that though Hotspur may be forgiven, his elders never will be. It is both noble and ironic that Hotspur rides forth to his death proclaiming the name and motto of his house. In spite of him the unity of the Percy family fails its supreme test.

Hotspur's character is controlled by the nature of his heritage. Like Hal he grows to be morally superior to the older generation of his family (indeed, he shows this superiority sooner and more obviously than Hal), but he can be virtuous only at the cost of a crippling innocence. While his father and uncle tangle themselves in nets of their own plotting, the world is very simple for him. Military honor and family loyalty are the two poles of his nature. Unlike Hal he never has to separate himself from his family because he does not even perceive the difference between them and himself. The charm of his integrity is great, but the integrity toward which Hal is working is more impressive simply because it takes more into account. Somewhere there is an ethical ideal that allows for the necessities of political calculation, and the perfect king must find that kind of ideal if he is not to fall into quixotism, the vice in Hotspur's virtue.

Insofar as Henry IV embodies true royalty and order, he is a model by which Hal can grow, but because of his guilt Henry is never at ease in the tension between ideals and policy. Hotspur offers a pattern of military chivalry to Hal and a rival whom he must overcome and transcend, but he too offers no final model. Even his thoroughly delightful marriage falls short of full maturity. Though he and his wife adore each other, their relationship has something of a boy and girl playing at marriage.[12] In short, he is another Mercutio, full of the charm of a limited nature. The final verdict of the play, reinforced by the symbolic tableau of Hal standing over Hotspur's body, is that he is not a sufficient pattern for the Prince of Wales. He cannot complete the redemption of the new generation because his ties are to a deeply corrupt part of the old and because he escapes his heritage only into a world of fantasy, where the simple absolutes of childhood become the standards of men.

Falstaff and the family.—Falstaff also illuminates Hal's relationship with his father. This is only one part of his significance, but he does function as an inverted parallel to Hotspur and a parody of Henry IV. If Hotspur is youth refusing to accept a fully human maturity, Falstaff is old age masquerading as youth.[13] He turns everything unpleasant into a pleasant fiction: old age into the effect of too much piety, highway robbers into "Diana's foresters" (I.ii.25), and cowardice into a lion's instinct. The measure of his wit is the artistry with which he keeps this artificial world going. Hal's wit characteristically tests that world against reality and points out the ludicrous incongruity of the two. Our pleasure in Falstaff is the exhilaration of freedom, and Shakespeare's craft prevents us from noticing how meaningless that freedom can be. Falstaff revolts not against the older generation but against his place in that generation. As a result, he can teach Hal a route of escape from his father, but not how to put meaning into that escape.

Falstaff becomes specifically relevant to the theme

of fathers and sons when he makes himself a parody
of Henry IV or, alternatively, of Hal to Hal's Henry.
Both poses run through his conversations with Hal.
His mimicking of Puritan cant suggests that he is a
sage, paternal figure whose counsel Hal should follow. Thus Hal should overcome his youthful wayward-
ness and turn to the vocation of highway robbery;
Falstaff says to Poins: "Well, God give thee the spirit
of persuasion, and him the ears of profiting, that what
thou speakest may move, and what he hears may be
believed" (I.ii.147-49). But not many lines earlier Falstaff is a prodigal corrupted by a devilish young
prince: "O, thou hast damnable iteration, and art indeed able to corrupt a saint: thou hast done much
harm upon me, Hal, God forgive thee for it" (88-90).
This theme is summed up when he and Hal stage two
impromptu dramas on the lecture from his father that
hangs over Hal. A closer examination of this scene
should illustrate how the Falstaff plot sheds light on
the relationship between Hal and Henry IV.

It is astonishing that Shakespeare can parody in advance one of the most moving scenes of the play without destroying its effect. All the elements of the formal
Henry IV are in Falstaff's parody. Henry's severely
rhetorical style is broadened into a parody-version of
John Lyly's stilted moralizing. Using that mode, Falstaff burlesques the code of aristocratic birth in the
course of his sermon:

> That thou art my son I have partly thy mother's word,
> partly my own opinion, but chiefly a villainous trick of
> thine eye, and a foolish hanging of thy nether lip, that

doth warrant me. If then thou be son to me, here lies the point—why, being son to me, art thou so pointed at? Shall the blessed sun of heaven prove a micher, and eat blackberries? A question not to be asked. Shall the son of England prove a thief, and take purses? A question to be asked.

(II.iv.397-406)

Noblesse oblige is not what marks this inheritance; rather it is "a villainous trick of thine eye, a foolish hanging of thy nether lip" that Hal shares with his father. The sun, that sacred image of royalty, becomes a truant schoolboy picking blackberries, as Falstaff toys with the serious pun on sun/son common in the lore of royal inheritance. (Compare, for example, *Richard III*, I.iii.263-69.) Even Henry's tears are foreshadowed in Falstaff's antitheses: "Harry, now I do not speak to thee in drink, but in tears; not in pleasure, but in passion; not in words only, but in woes also" (410-12). Only the severe dignity of the real confrontation between Hal and his father, the quiet means by which it expresses its deep-felt emotions, could save it from this parody-in-advance.

A more serious parallel between Falstaff and Henry IV emerges when the knight uses both his acting roles to defend his "virtuous" companionship with Hal. Behind the joke of it is Falstaff's constant desire to make a claim on Hal's friendship. Henry is hurt because he does not understand the nature of Hal's desire to flee the court; so Falstaff looks with mingled hope and doubt toward the future because he misjudges Hal. Neither of the old men is quite willing to allow Hal his independence, and so both stand in the way of his growth toward full maturity. In a passage too often emended, Falstaff suggests this theme unconsciously. Continuing his defense of "that Falstaff" while the sheriff knocks at the door, he says to Hal, "Never call a true piece of gold a counterfeit: thou art essentially made without seeming so" (485-87).[14] That is, Falstaff's virtue and worth live untainted under the disreputable appearances of his exterior just as Hal's royalty is hidden but not obliterated by his youthful pranks. Falstaff uses the figure of coins being stamped to suggest one Renaissance view of moral aristocracy: like pure gold, inherited virtue cannot be corrupted by external circumstances. But it is precisely this fact about Hal that makes Falstaff's eventual rejection certain.

This consequence is likewise implicit in the symbolic tableau at Shrewsbury when Hal stands above the bodies of Hotspur and Falstaff, the two half-men whom he has transcended. Of course Falstaff is not really dead (though presumably the audience does not know that when he falls under Douglas's sword); still Hal can never be so close to him as before. When in the impromptu play Hal symbolically takes the role of his father and banishes the eloquent knight with his final "I do, I will" (475), the outcome is already clear. Falstaff is only a mock father, and so when Hal must turn to the serious business of his life, the fat knight can be nothing to him. This element is only one dark thread in the delightful pattern of comedy that II.iv provides, but it is there, a clear statement of the serious theme of the play.[15]

Hal stands at the center of *1 Henry IV*, poised between Hotspur and Falstaff. Through his rivalry with Hotspur, he enters the public realm of the play, the war of the Percy rebellion. Through his association with Falstaff, he enters a realm of tavern brawls and highway robbery. Both sides are relevant to the central theme of the play, Hal's growth toward readiness for kingship. What gives this theme its pattern, the controlling myth of Hal's growth, is the Prodigal Son story of a king and prince. From this point of view the crisis of the play is Hal's confrontation with his father in III.ii. Their reconciliation in that scene provides the turning point not only in their relationship but also in the destinies of Hotspur and Falstaff. Conversely these two figures provide a commentary on Hal and Henry IV by their words and by ironic parallels of which they are not fully conscious. *1 Henry IV* is a rich and diverse play, but these thematic bonds help to give it a strong orderliness and pattern.

2 Henry IV

In many ways *2 Henry IV* is an amplified repetition of themes from the previous play, yet both tone and emphasis are much changed. The Prodigal Son pattern reappears, but with less importance, partly because Hal and his father are less central figures. Hal first appears in II.ii and Henry not until III.i. Even in Hal's story there is another morality pattern of almost equal importance, the Psychomachia, with Falstaff and the Lord Chief Justice cast as vice and virtue warring for the prince's soul.[16] That theme itself is only partly developed since their relationship to Hal is not fully dramatized. Falstaff expands beyond such a role so as nearly to take over the play on his own account, and the Lord Chief Justice has too little dramatic importance to justify his symbolic weight. The same tripartite division of plots as in *1 Henry IV* occurs here, but the connections among them are at the same time more schematic and less powerful. Indeed, the primary unity of *2 Henry IV* is tonal: all three plots reinforce the impression of an old and dying land looking with mingled hope and fear at the impending change to a new generation. In the richness and variety of its individual scenes and characters, *2 Henry IV* is almost equal to its predecessor, but only the tonal pattern gives coherence to the rather sprawling whole.

This picture of a dying generation and the growth of a new one to succeed it is the most panoramic expression of Shakespeare's concern with fathers and sons. The initial dramatic impression is one of age and decay.[17] First we see the aged Northumberland's crafty sickness and then Falstaff's even less elegant ailment (whether syphilis or gout). But the primary symbolic fact of the play is the king's illness, which a number of the characters discuss before he appears "in his nightgown" (stage direction at III.i.1). The land declines in sympathy with its sick and dying king until its omens mark his imminent death.[18] The waning vigor of most of the characters creates an air of impersonality in which superhuman forces rather than strong personalities seem to control events. In such a world an abstraction like Vergil's *Fama* is appropriate, and she appears in the Induction as "Rumour painted full of tongues" (stage direction at 1). Rumor's imagery recalls the more vigorous world of *1 Henry IV* when she reports that the king

> Hath beaten down young Hotspur and his troops,
> Quenching the flame of bold rebellion
> Even with the rebels' blood.
>
> (25-27)

In contrast with this bold violence in the past is the scene to come, set in a "worm-eaten hold of ragged stone" (Induction, 35), where an old man lies feigning sickness to avoid the battle in which his son has died.

What other Shakespearian play is so full of old, sick men who fear or long for death? Yet at the same time there is another quality even in some of the old men themselves. After all, Falstaff is one of them, and his explanation for his aged appearance contains some truth behind the impudent fantasy: "My lord, I was born about three of the clock in the afternoon, with a white head, and something a round belly. For my voice, I have lost it with hallooing, and singing of anthems" (I.ii.186-89). He shows the external signs of old age without its deficiencies. Justice Shallow is the epitome of age with his often-repeated and mendacious recollections of youth, his folly only barely covered by cunning, and his feeble pride in his land and wealth. Yet even he is associated with those ancient pastoral symbols of regeneration and growth, farming and raising flocks. If the king is sick unto death, his land still has reserves of vitality. Though less obviously than in *1 Henry IV,* English life preserves something of its normal state, the quality that allows it to re-generate itself while the court declines under the strain of opposing the forces of disorder.

In such a world Hal appears subdued to the taint of those around him, his reformation in *1 Henry IV* rather arbitrarily forgotten by the court. Shakespeare again follows the Prodigal Son pattern but changes its tone by use of a familiar motif, the king or prince in disguise.[19] This device is common in Elizabethan drama, as in the two popular plays *George à Greene* and *Friar Bacon and Friar Bungay.*[20] Its dramatic appeal is clear: it suggests the essential oneness of monarch and people since in disguise he can associate with them as equals. The king, that austere embodiment of glory and justice, is also a "king of good fellows," as Henry V calls himself while wooing Katherine (V.ii. 256). Yet implicit in disguise is the other side. Only when he is unrecognized, only as Harry LeRoy, can the king be just a good fellow among the people. In his own name he is the ruler, sacred, untouchable, and lonely, with all the pathos Shakespeare gives to that loneliness.

Hal literally puts on a disguise when he and Poins transform themselves into drawers in order to spy on Falstaff. Hal comments sardonically on the effect: "From a god to a bull? A heavy descension! It was Jove's case. From a prince to a prentice? A low trans-formation, that shall be mine, for in everything the purpose must weigh with the folly" (II.ii.166-69).[21] Hal's disguise allows him to hear Falstaff picturing him in ordinary terms indeed, but the knight's description is as usual unrelated to truth, as he admits when Hal reveals himself. The physical disguise stands for no inner degradation, though it represents the whole land's opinion of Hal.

Hal's self-concealment, however, is not primarily physical. Shakespeare gives him a moral disguise so that all around him misjudge his nature. Hal is consistently ironic, aware of the discrepancy between what he seems and what he will prove to be. He can descend to be a drawer because the genuine Hal stands back and comments. The ingenuity of this device is that it leaves ambiguous just what the real Hal is and so makes the conversion both dramatic and plausible. Warwick portrays Hal as wholly untainted, if rather calculating for most tastes:

> The Prince but studies his companions
> Like a strange tongue, wherein, to gain the language,
> 'Tis needful that the most immodest word
> Be look'd upon and learnt; which once attain'd,
> Your Highness knows, comes to no further use
> But to be known and hated.
>
> > (IV.iv.68-73)

The implication of this speech is that there can be no real bond between a king and lower men, that he must know them only to reject them.[22] Yet Warwick seems to be reassuring the old king in the face of his own less sanguine view. He is as gloomy as the rest when Hal succeeds to the throne (V.ii.14-18). If Hal's disguise is just policy, he has deceived everyone.

Surely, however, the truth is more complex. Shakespeare uses disguise ambiguously in his plays: it both conceals and manifests identity. Rosalind and Viola hide their femininity in boys' clothes, yet both can express their natures even more fully for their disguises. In donning a friar's robes and acting as spiritual guide, the Duke in *Measure for Measure* adopts the sacred equivalent of his secular position, and the two roles enrich each other. In the same way, Hal manifests himself in disguise, even frees a part of his nature that the court stifles. Not only does he escape its formality and develop the oneness with his kingdom that is the basis of true royalty, but he gets beyond the guilt of his inheritance by renewed contact with the people, the source of royal power and right.

More than in *1 Henry IV*, Shakespeare points this play toward the confrontation of the royal father and son. Until IV.v, when they come together, they appear separately. When Hal enters, he appears subdued to the over-all tone of gloom and decline. He has just returned from fighting the rebels, and he reveals shortly that he is grieving at his father's illness. Shrewsbury seems to have solved nothing. He is terribly conscious of his ordinary humanity, the obverse of his royal position. He can laugh at this side of himself and almost regains his spirits in wittily describing Poins's linen, but his companion's inadequacy makes itself obvious just then. Poins uses Henry's illness as a weapon in their battle of wits, oblivious to the sincerity of Hal's sorrow. Shakespeare transfers to this companion the feelings of Hal himself in *The Famous Victories of Henry the Fifth*.[23] Poins's jesting drives

Hal further into his characteristic irony, and the irony now has a tone of self-contempt that embitters his wit.

Hal tells Poins that he is seeking London pleasures rather than attending his ill father because he does not want to seem like a hypocrite. Although these words show that he is not insensitive to his father's illness, he is once again rationalizing his wildness, as he did in the *1 Henry IV* soliloquy. He flees from his grief into dissipation, and so a companion like Poins necessarily misunderstands him. Because Hal is conscious of his irresponsibility, his irony remains strongly active. Falstaff's suggestion that he is to marry Poins's sister merely amuses him, though it throws Poins into confusion. But even his highest spirits are tainted with an uneasy self-consciousness. Thus he turns from the laughter at Falstaff's letter to a biblical-euphuistic reflection in Falstaff's own vein: "Well, thus we play the fools with the time, and the spirits of the wise sit in the clouds and mock us" (134-35).

Through the whole of II.ii runs a constant play on the themes of noble birth, kinship, and marriage. Poins hypothesizes imperviousness to mortal discomfort in Hal, "one of so high blood" (3), and ridicules Falstaff's pride in his knighthood, comparing it to the vanity of the king's relatives. Still he is quick to defend himself as no worse than "a second brother" (63) when Hal links him with Falstaff as a corrupter of the true prince. Hal praises him for strengthening the family by producing bastards. The page contributes a descent for Bardolph to explain his red nose and a kinship between Falstaff and Doll Tearsheet, which Hal promptly sets in its true light: "Even such kin as

the parish heifers are to the town bull" (149-50). Inheritance, kinship, and marriage in both high and low
life seem like the tawdry shifts of a fallen world. As
Hal reduces himself from a prince to a drawer, so
marriage degenerates to a coupling of bull and heifer.
But Hal's ironic detachment saves him from being
deeply tainted by this debasement of human values.
He is consciously playing a witty game while reserv-
ing part of himself out of his companions' view.

When Hal meets Falstaff, the knight describes his
degeneration beneath his princely forebears (not
knowing of Hal's presence): "A would have made a
good pantler, a would ha' chipped bread well" (II.iv.
234-35). He calls Hal "a bastard son of the King's"
(280). Here the idea of Hal's degeneracy is reduced
to Falstaffian absurdity and thus banished. If Hal's
anger at Falstaff is feigned, his debasement to drawer
—or tavern-companion—is equally unreal. When a sum-
mons to duty comes, his spirits rally with a dignity
opposite which Falstaff's pose of high responsibility is
both comic and slightly contemptible. Thus Hal is
never really threatened with attraction into Falstaff's
orbit in 2 Henry IV, though he is swayed by the need
to escape his responsibilities and grief while he still
can.

Poised opposite this scene is Henry IV's first appearance, opening with his powerful soliloquy on the
cares of sleepless royalty. This episode continues the
pattern of aging men striving toward unreal goals. Hal
turns with renewed vigor toward his future as he
leaves Falstaff, but Henry falls into the old man's trap

of seeing time on so large a scale that men's efforts appear useless:

> O, if this were seen,
> The happiest youth, viewing his progress through,
> What perils past, what crosses to ensue,
> Would shut the book and sit him down and die.
> (III.i.53-56)

His words compel an expansion of the dramatic horizons to take in more time, especially since he goes on to recall the origins of this upheaval, the events recorded in *Richard II*. His melancholy conceals from him any hint of his son's future glory, though in a still longer view his words evoke the whole pattern that the first tetralogy completes, with Henry V's early death and the loss of all his conquests. In such a broad view of history individual men, even kings, become tiny figures. Warwick merely reinforces this conclusion when he explains Richard's successful prophecy by the operation of historical necessity. Henry argues from these thoughts a code of fatalism, the only basis for responsible action in a determined world.

Thus the king shares with the rebels and Justice Shallow a fascination with the past and an obsession with the future. His plans show the irrational fluctuations of a sick man. He clings to his planned crusade to the Holy Land, which he must know will never come about, but which to him stands for escape from the disorder of the land. When in the wanderings of his illness he comes to a more realistic concern for the future, he broods over what will happen to England with Hal's accession. There is nothing of this concern in III.i, but in IV.iv it forms the prelude to his confrontation with Hal. His first analysis of his son is not at all unperceptive; as far as it goes, it describes Hal's character in both this play and the next. When he advises Clarence how to strengthen the bonds of family with the new king, he draws on the tradition that ideal kings counsel with their kin, who far surpass the usual favorites in loyalty and disinterestedness. In combining this ideal with psychological acuity, Henry appears at his best.

The information that Hal is dining with his tavern companions throws his father into a quite different mood. The king is hurt by Hal's apparent callousness in enjoying himself while Henry lies ill. He can still see in his son "the noble image of my youth" (IV.iv. 55), the hereditary representative of his own heroic young manhood; but at the same time his personal anguish expands into a gloomy view of the future for England. Hal will be a typical weak king, like Richard II counseled by "rage and hot blood" (63). As he destroys the kingdom, his father, the symbol of lost order, will be "sleeping with my ancestors" (61). In this way the theme of the prince's wildness and redemption is brought forward and his relationship with his father made the vehicle for showing his growth, as in *1 Henry IV*.

The theme receives a new coloring from Henry's nearness to death. He represents an old and dying generation, desperately afraid that it has failed to pass on to the new the traditional morality that is the basis of civilization. The omens mentioned by Gloucester and Clarence are ambiguous in that they suggest an impending breach in nature, but at the same time are a continuing, cyclic natural process. They are of "Unfather'd heirs and loathly births of nature" (122), but they are part of a recurrent pattern, recalling the time "That our great-grandsire Edward sick'd and died" (128). That is the paradox of "The king is dead; long live the king!" The break in order is at the same time part of a larger order. Henry is no more than one link in the great historic process, a momentary and sicklied perception of which has thrown him into despairing fatalism.

It is ironic that in the final misunderstanding Henry attacks Hal for what has been great filial propriety. His sitting by the bed is a traditional office of affection.[24] The similarity between his soliloquy on the crown and his father's meditation on sleep indicates the fundamental harmony of the two men. Hal's words are a perfect balance of filial grief and the consciousness of orderly inheritance:

> Thy due from me
> Is tears and heavy sorrows of the blood,
> Which nature, love, and filial tenderness
> Shall, O dear father, pay thee plenteously.
> My due from thee is this imperial crown,
> Which, as immediate from thy place and blood,
> Derives itself to me.
>
> (IV.v.36-42)

His grief is "of the blood," both deeply felt and natural, moved by the bond of kinship. At the same time he takes on with proper dignity the "lineal honour" (45) of his new royalty. He shows that like his father he is concerned with the pattern of succession, which will in time invest his son with the same kingship. Thus Hal behaves properly in both his public and private roles, as son and as prince.

Henry's rage when he wakes to find the crown gone finally clears the air between the two. There is a moving irony in his exclamation:

> See, sons, what things you are,
> How quickly nature falls into revolt
> When gold becomes her object!
>
> (64-66)

The audience has just seen that to Hal the crown is a symbol of inherited responsibility. Henry in his anger reduces it to mere gold, the object of greed. He pictures himself and his son stripped of their royalty, a merchant and his wastrel heir. He associates himself with the "foolish over-careful fathers" (67) of classical comedy and its descendants. Calmed somewhat by Warwick's report of Hal's sorrow, he still falls back on the petulant question, "But wherefore did he take away the crown?" (88). Under the weight of his sickness and anger, he behaves as he never has in public before, without concern for his royal dignity.

Henry begins his accusation with an expression of his most intimate feeling, fear that Hal hates him and wants his death. He gives this mood the most terrible of expressions, the image of a son murdering his father:

Thou hid'st a thousand daggers in thy thoughts,
Which thou hast whetted on thy stony heart,
To stab at half an hour of my life.

(106-8)

But with his figure converting Hal's tears to coronation balm, his thoughts turn from himself to the welfare of his kingdom. As man he is a forgotten father,
and as king he is a rejected symbol of order:

Pluck down my officers; break my decrees;
For now a time is come to mock at form.

(117-18)

He speaks for the expectations of his people, or at
least their fears, to judge from the gloomy conversations in the court that open V.ii and from Falstaff and
Pistol's hopes for the new reign. He sees as a consequence of Hal's accession the same apocalyptic collapse of order that Northumberland evokes in his grief
at Hotspur's death (I.i.153-60).

Once again as in *1 Henry IV*, Hal must justify himself to his father. The tact and dignity with which he
does so are convincing proof of his moral readiness
for his approaching duties. He can allude only briefly
to his purposed reformation as king, since the most
serious charge against him is that he anticipates that
time too eagerly. But the real source of Henry's pain
is Hal's apparent lack of filial love. In reply Hal uses
the language of family rectitude, showing his commitment to the order of the family. He makes his kneeling for pardon a symbol of "my most inward true and

duteous spirit" (147) and even his taking the crown "The quarrel of a true inheritor" (168) against its cruelty. In the latter explanation he can tell only half the truth since a father hungering for love does not want to be told of his son's self-confident readiness to replace him in the succession of royalty. (Contrast Hal's actual words at 40-46 with his report of them in 158-64.) Hal strikes exactly the right note in showing his awareness of the cares surrounding the crown. The words proclaim sympathetic affection for his father while proving that he is not excessively ambitious. That is not to say that he is hypocritically playing on his father's emotions. The genuineness of his love is shown both by his tears and by his dignified but pointed references to his own grief.

In spite of his capacity for ironic detachment, Hal is more than a coldly pragmatic politician. He has succeeded in ordering the public and private claims of his life. He can express his affections in such a way that they support his official role rather than undermining it. The passionate relief of Henry's reply shows how successful Hal's defense has been. He appreciates Hal's judgment as well as his affection, and so he opens his political stratagems more plainly than ever before. For the first time a less than penitential motive for his projected crusade to the Holy Land emerges, and he counsels Hal to imitate this plan by stimulating "foreign quarrels" (214). His guilt has immersed him in the disorder that perpetuates itself, though his very understanding of the situation shows that in some degree he has gone beyond the guilt. Whereas he seized the throne, Hal is successive heir, but that can be so only because Henry is indeed king. Hal can claim the throne simply and unequivocally, as his father could never do.[25] That is the source of strength by which he surpasses his father, whose intricate political schemes and vague quest for purgation end with the grotesque irony of his death in the Jerusalem Chamber, not in the holy city of Jerusalem.

As in *1 Henry IV*, the private reconciliation with his father leads to a public expression of Hal's worth. In the earlier play he embodies chivalric heroism at Shrewsbury, and in this he gives public assent to the virtue of justice, the final measure of a king. When the Lord Chief Justice discusses the old king's death with Warwick and Henry's younger sons, all of them look forward with dread to the new reign. The newly crowned Henry V enters and senses their fear, which he sets out with fine tact to allay. He treats his brothers as fellows in a family, but also as representatives of a royal heritage. Now he is both their king and head of their family:

> For me, by heaven, I bid you be assur'd,
> I'll be your father and your brother too;
> Let me but bear your love, I'll bear your cares.
>
> (V.ii.56-58)

Thus Hal shows that he is concerned to maintain the unity of his family, as his father was before him.

When he turns to the gloomy Lord Chief Justice, a bit of his old ironic humor comes out, albeit subdued to his new dignity. He allows the old man to think that he is still angry at having been imprisoned

and so draws forth an impassioned defense of the rule
of justice over all men, even a prince:

> Be now the father, and propose a son,
> Hear your own dignity so much profan'd,
> See your most dreadful laws so loosely slighted,
> Behold yourself so by a son disdain'd:
> And then imagine me taking your part,
> And in your power soft silencing your son.
>
> (V.ii.92-97)

By giving Hal a significant imaginary role, the Chief
Justice teaches that one cannot violate the laws of the
state without breaking the whole moral order, even
the bonds of family. All the more must a prince submit to the laws of a king who is his father. Hence his
severe justice has been a defense of fatherhood as well
as law in the state. Hal accepts this truth for himself
and his posterity. Declaring to the Lord Chief Justice,
"You shall be as a father to my youth" (118), he takes
the total responsibility of his vocation. Hal has become
Henry V, both a king and a man. If he must reject
Falstaff and the pleasures of his youth in order to take
up his new role, he firmly does so as he turns to the
emblem of kingly justice.

The Decay of the Percy Rebellion.—The other two
plots of *2 Henry IV* are less fully relevant to this theme
than their counterparts in *1 Henry IV*. The episodes of
the Percy rebellion are a strangely disjointed tale with
no Hotspur to give them focus, but parts of this plot
are related to the theme of father and son. In this

play of brooding on the past, Hotspur's fate is one obsessive memory to the Percies. Northumberland's wild grief at his son's death is genuine enough, though the poetry is in the old style of formal artificiality. This quality takes on symbolic overtones at one point in his lament:

> Let heaven kiss earth! Now let not Nature's hand
> Keep the wild flood confin'd! Let order die!
> And let this world no longer be a stage
> To feed contention in a ling'ring act;
> But let one spirit of the first-born Cain
> Reign in all bosoms.
>
> (I.i.153-58)

Here his sorrow at his son's death becomes an expression of the disorder that the Percy rebellion arouses. Guilt at his own betrayal and grief at his son's futile destruction lead him to an image of familial destruction. He invokes the fratricidal hatred of Cain to be the guiding principle of the universe. Extravagant though his outcry is, it suits a world in which political disorder has produced a breach in nature, so that old men live on while their heirs die before reaching maturity.[26]

Hotspur's widow returns to this theme of broken paternal bonds while trying to persuade Northumberland to flee to Scotland. She is a helpless victim of political strife, like Lady Blanche in *King John,* but she is also a voice of his conscience as she reminds him of Hotspur's virtues. It is bitterly appropriate that her recollections of her husband's glory serve only to unnerve his father so that he once again betrays his party by fleeing a crucial battle. In her brooding on Hotspur, Lady Percy has some of Constance's intensity without her mad excessiveness, and Northumberland is as clumsy and weakly Machiavellian as King Philip. Shakespeare is at some pains to show the family life of the rebel group by this scene (II.iii), so that he may contrast that of the court as he did in *1 Henry IV*. While the House of Lancaster overcomes the tensions within it to unite behind a king who carries on his father's name and glory, the House of the Percies has collapsed into disorder memorialized by the laments of women and old men.

During the confrontation at Gaultree (IV.i-iii), the oratory of both sides is full of family allusions in the old manner. Most ominous of these is Hastings's all-too-accurate prediction:

> And though we here fall down,
> We have supplies to second our attempt:
> If they miscarry, theirs shall second them;
> And so success of mischief shall be born,
> And heir from heir shall hold this quarrel up
> Whiles England shall have generation.
>
> (IV.ii.44-49)

This is the perverted inheritance that dominates the Henry VI plays. Calamity ("mischief") is to thrive by a monstrous succession, to multiply itself out of this conflict like the heads of a Hydra (38). Earlier the Archbishop describes the condition of the state as a disease that only rebellion can cure (IV.i.53-66). When

Mowbray derives his quarrel from his father, Bolingbroke's enemy in *Richard II,* and Prince John wages
war in his father's name, the pattern of generations
trapped in an endless quarrel has already begun. There
is a terrible weariness in the Archbishop's explanation
that the king will be glad to compromise in order to
avoid breeding new quarrels with the heirs of the
defeated rebels. All these men are oppressed by the
futility of their actions, yet they must go on as though
they believed in their cause.

If England were doomed to choose between its sick,
aging king and these rebels, it would have little hope
for the future. Prince John, however, is more difficult to
evaluate. He is part of the younger, more vigorous generation, and Hal has praised his valor at Shrewsbury.
His poise in command and the skill with which he out-
wits the rebels show him to be a formidable general.
Falstaff's soliloquy at the end of IV.iii makes this brother
still another figure to be compared with Hal. Falstaff
laments, "Good faith, this same young sober-blooded
boy doth not love me, nor a man cannot make him
laugh" (85-87). He suggests that, unlike his brother,
Hal has enriched "the cold blood he did naturally inherit
of his father" (116-17) by judicious use of sack. This
comic justification for drinking should not conceal his
perception of a genuine difference between these two
sons of one father, a difference expressed by Hal's affection for Falstaff.

Although there is nothing that requires a general to
keep faith with rebels, John's use of equivocation, the
Jesuits' technique, cannot have endeared him to an
Elizabethan audience; and surely we are not forced to

admire the glib piety of his comment on the success of his stratagem: "God, and not we, hath safely fought today" (IV.ii.121).[27] His unsmiling virtue comes perilously close to smugness. He lacks his brother's *sprezzatura*, Hal's ability to carry his virtues lightly. That is why Hal can be amused and generous when Falstaff pretends to heroic merit, and John can only proclaim a generosity he shows no signs of having. Hence John is no more than his father's son, but Hal is the future hero of Agincourt, a king who can inspire by being both a heroic model and a good fellow.

Falstaff in Decline.—Falstaff is less closely related to the family theme in this play than in *1 Henry IV*, though in the process of degrading him Shakespeare emphasizes his sterility, his isolation from the normal processes of marriage and rearing a family. Seeing him with the prostitute Doll Tearsheet in his lap, Poins exclaims (perhaps unfairly, if Doll's testimony can be trusted): "Is it not strange that desire should so many years outlive performance?" (II.iv.258-59). The fat knight, who has been jesting about marriage and avoiding it for years (as in I.ii.241-43), can move the sentimental tears of a whore; but all his wit cannot hide the barrenness of his life. Even Shallow and Silence have children of whom to exchange news, and Shallow inquires after Falstaff's wife when Bardolph arrives on the recruiting trip. Falstaff is an outsider to all family bonds, in that way resembling Richard III. As with Richard, this detachment gives his wit the freedom to play freely over the family. His unfettered vision lets him see that "the son of the female is the shadow of the male; it is often so indeed—but much of the father's substance!" (III.ii.129-31).[28] He can even view the inheritance of Henry IV's sons with healthy cynicism. His wit breaks through orthodox doctrine to allow a fuller understanding of the difference between Hal and John, but he pushes his analysis no further than a jesting metaphor.

The comparison with Richard III does not go very far, of course, since Falstaff is by no means the same threat to the family. If we distinguish between the two sides of the Vice, jester and devil,[29] Falstaff parallels the former and Richard the latter. In the symbolic pattern of the play, Falstaff embodies the semi-authorized detachment from orthodox values to which figures like the comic Vice and the Lord of Misrule give public expression. If one were to take Mistress Quickly's suffering seriously, then he would be a monster, but Shakespeare uses her absurdities to divert attention from the pathos of her situation. Also, Falstaff is more vulnerable than Richard III. Unmoved by his mother's curse, Richard finds a worthy antagonist only in the whole force of Providence. Falstaff is susceptible to the griefs of old age and (though this is more lightly touched) of loneliness. An empty old man, he is forced to make claims on his youthful friend's affections, claims that Hal's position makes it impossible to honor. Hence there is a sharp pathos in his appeal to the new king, selfish though it may be, and in Hal's blunt reply:

Fal. My King! My Jove! I speak to thee, my heart!
King. I know thee not, old man.

(V.v.46-47)

Here at a serious level is Hal's constant reply to Falstaff's fantastic wit, the test of reality. Falstaff can be nothing to the king, neither father nor companion; he is simply an old man.[30]

One must neither ignore nor exaggerate the pain of this rejection. Falstaff is hurt more deeply than in his hopes of advancement, yet he is not crushed. Like the figure that rose from the apparently fatal battle with Douglas, he turns to Justice Shallow and puts off his creditor with his usual bland unscrupulousness: "Master Shallow, I owe you a thousand pound" (73).[31] Whatever Shakespeare's plans for the knight's future, it seems clear that he is hopelessly estranged from the king, but not destroyed. The Lord of Misrule both dies and lives forever; the isolated man has given no hostages to fortune. As for the new king, he has to reject Falstaff in order to accept his symbolic father, the Lord Chief Justice. Still the critics' nagging sense of inadequacy in this scene has some justification.[32] The main awkwardness comes from the thin dramatic presence of the Lord Chief Justice, who makes only the most perfunctory opposite to Falstaff. Henry V's character suffers in many eyes because he chooses a symbol over a full-blooded dramatic character with symbolic overtones, but at the symbolic level the intent is clear: he chooses justice and family order over anarchy and disorder, the effects of a king who submits his state to selfish favorites. He chooses the wisdom of age, not the folly of age masquerading as youth. He chooses a man who can be a father to him as just king, not a man to whom fatherhood is only a joke.

Conclusion: 1 and 2 Henry IV

The two parts of *Henry IV* show with the fullness of great dramatic art Hal's development into a hero-king, the embodiment of glory based on order and justice. While England overcomes the principle of disorder in the Percy rebellion, a man develops into a king who will for a time offer the ideal alternative to disorder: union under a banner of patriotic glory and national purpose. Hal's moral growth is shown as a series of decisions in which he accepts what is good in the various models proposed to him and resists their vices and weaknesses. Thus he finds a genuine heritage, his roots in the past, and at the same time goes beyond it.

Shakespeare gives depth to this theme by showing it at several levels. First, with human psychology he portrays a son who pulls away from his father to declare his independence and then is reconciled when his father comes to accept that independence and he accepts the responsibilities of his freedom. Because Shakespeare's blank verse and prose have become flexible enough to suggest the tones of normal speech without being subdued to the commonplace, he can catch the humanity of his king and prince with uncanny precision. At the same time he can suggest symbolic levels. Most important of these is the underlying pattern of the Prodigal Son story, which not only universalizes Hal's situation but gives it a religious overtone. To the Elizabethans a king was an earthly god in more than a purely figurative sense, a type of the King of Heaven. To them the story of the Prodigal Son had a secular, educational meaning, but also its primary religious significance. Thus Hal is both a son reconciled with his father and a soul reconciled with the principle of order and virtue in the universe. Finally, Shakespeare uses the relationship of Henry IV and Hal to suggest a theme that runs through his whole career: the redemption of a sinful older generation by the idealism and faith of a new one. If Hal does not have the symbolic resonance of Perdita, still a sick land is revived by his accession, and the glory of Agincourt lies ahead of a kingdom only just emerging from civil war.[33]

The Elizabethans were as conscious as we of concrete reality, of things and men in themselves. At the same time, however, they saw things and men as expressions of a whole, as parts in a divinely ordered pattern. The family corresponds to the state, not just as a quaint figure of speech, but because in some mysterious but real way the king is indeed a father, the subject a son, and order in the family the same as political justice. In following this mental habit of his age, Shakespeare learns how to combine the public and the personal in one dramatic structure. Because he sees similarity of pattern where we see difference of content, he can unite ideal and actual, the symbolic and the realistic. To solve this problem for the family and the state is not to solve it for all of his drama, but the solution illustrated in the Henry IV plays points toward the even more complex handling of similar problems in the great tragedies.

Taking this view of the Henry IV plays implies one answer to a serious critical issue. If the family is essentially parallel to the state and Henry V's royalty dependent on his successful growth as a son and brother, then Derek Traversi's argument that becoming a king involves sacrificing part of one's humanity must be wrong.[34] The whole tenor of this chapter has suggested that, but it may be worthwhile to state the issue in more abstract terms. Traversi's view springs from an important truth about Shakespeare's handling of kingship, that he emphasizes the king's isolation and consequent loneliness. In giving up Falstaff, Henry V is making a sacrifice. Does it follow, however, that he is less of a man for doing so? In part the question is one of definition, whether or not being a man involves cultivating openness and spontaneity over dignity and responsibility. But there is an issue of interpretation involved as well: is Hal as king or as prince cold and heartless? Does he play with Falstaff's feelings for purely utilitarian ends and then reject him without regret? Since Hal is necessarily playing the public role of newly crowned king in the rejection scene, we cannot tell with precisely what feelings he rejects Falstaff, and the disguise motif leaves even his earlier feelings veiled. Still, this chapter has suggested some reasons for rejecting the idea that Hal is from the beginning a coldblooded plotter. It also has suggested that Prince John is a contrast to Hal, not a parallel that Falstaff ironically misunderstands. Hence it seems reasonable to view Hal's growth from prince to king as paralleled by a growth from boy to man.

Whatever one's view of the Henry IV plays, no one denies that they manifest Shakespeare's dramatic maturity as none of the earlier history plays do. Something in the material at his disposal—chronicles of old civil wars, a crude dramatization of a wild prince's reformation, all the scores of known and unknown sources that flow together in the two plays—releases his imagination as even Sir Thomas More's imaginative portrayal of Richard III and the diverse materials behind *Richard II* had not done. This chapter has attempted to show how one theme, the relation of the family to the problems of state, shares in that sudden expansion of dramatic vision.

[1] Most scholars date the two plays between 1595 and 1598, though there are the usual theories of revision from an earlier form. See the summaries of these two problems in the New Variorum Editions, Samuel B. Hemingway's *Henry the Fourth Part I* (Philadelphia, 1936), and Matthias A. Shaaber's *The Second Part of Henry the Fourth* (Philadelphia, 1940), and G. Blakemore Evans's supplement to the former, the third issue of *Shakespeare Quarterly* 7 (1956). John Dover Wilson, "The Origins and Development of Shakespeare's *Henry IV*," *The Library* 4th ser., 26 (1945-46), 2-16, sets forth a theory of major revision. Another vexed issue is whether the two plays are to be considered discrete dramatic units or whether together they constitute a single ten-act play. John Dover Wilson, *The Fortunes of Falstaff* (Cambridge, Eng., 1943); E. M. W. Tillyard, *Shakespeare's History Plays* (New York, 1944); and A. R. Humphreys, *The Second Part of King Henry IV*, New Arden Edition (Cambridge, Mass., 1966), pp. xxi-xxviii, are important defenders of the unified plan. Among major arguments on the other side are M. A. Shaaber, "The Unity of *Henry IV*," *Joseph Quincy Adams Memorial Studies*, ed. James G. McManaway et al. (Washington, D.C., 1948), pp. 217-27; Harold Jenkins, *The Structural Problem in Shakespeare's Henry the Fourth* (London, 1956); and Robert Adger Law, "The Composition of Shakespeare's Lancastrian Trilogy," *Texas Studies in Literature and Language* 3 (1961), 321-27. Whatever the origin of the plays, they are clearly coordinated in theme, character, and action.

[2] For a general discussion of the Prodigal Son drama, see Chapter I, pp. 14-16. On the theme in *Henry IV*, see *The Fortunes of Falstaff*, pp. 17-25, and a reply by Peter Alexander, "Wilson on Falstaff," *Modern Language Review* 39 (1944), 408-9. Though most Renaissance educators are skeptical about wild youth's reforming, Henry Peacham is one exception. He even argues that "these of all other, if they be well tempered, proue the best metall" (*Peacham's Compleat Gentleman*, ed. G. S. Gordon [Oxford, Eng., 1906], p. 34).

[3] *1 Henry IV*, III.iii.77 (cf. Humphreys' note on the passage), IV.ii. 33-36; *2 Henry IV*, II.i.141-42.

[4] *The First Part of the History of Henry IV*, New Cambridge Shakespeare (Cambridge, Eng., 1946), note at I.i.1.

[5] Genesis 4:11; see Humphreys' note on the passage.

[6] William Empson discusses this episode in *English Pastoral Poetry* (New York, 1938), p. 44. However, to him it is an unequivocal condemnation of the king. Richard L. McGuire, "The Play-within-the-play in *1 Henry IV*," *Shakespeare Quarterly* 18 (1967), 52, points out that counterfeiting is a central image in the play, and James Winny, *The Player King: A Theme of Shakespeare's Histories* (New York, 1968), studies it at length.

[7] Quoted in New Variorum Edition, ed. Hemingway, note at I.ii.186.

[8] Cf. the discussion in Tillyard, pp. 278-80.

[9] "Behind Shakespeare's acceptance of a traditional story lies the sense, which grows as the action develops, that success in politics implies a moral loss, the sacrifice of more attractive qualities in the distinctively personal order" (Derek Traversi, *Shakespeare from Richard II to Henry V* [London, 1957], p. 58).

[10] "In this one instant, the disintegration of a family and the disintegration of a nation seem to have been simultaneously averted" (Alfred Harbage, *William Shakespeare: A Reader's Guide* [New York, 1963], p. 213).

[11] H. M. Richmond, *Shakespeare's Political Plays* (New York, 1967), p. 157, rather perversely attributes Hal's boldness to his knowledge that his father will not let him fight. Surely Vernon's report of the incident (V.ii.45-68) makes Hal's chivalric impressiveness clear.

[12] One would give much to have seen the impromptu play that Hal considers, with himself as Hotspur and "that damned brawn" Falstaff (II.iv.107-8) as Lady Percy.

[13] J. A. Bryant Jr., "Prince Hal and the Ephesians," *The Sewanee Review*, 62 (1959), 204-19, relates Falstaff to the Pauline "old man" and hence sees age as a symbol of unregenerate humanity. Cf. also D. J. Palmer, "Casting off the Old Man: History and St. Paul in 'Henry IV,'" *Critical Quarterly* 12 (1970), 267-83.

[14] The emendation of "made" to "mad" actually goes back to the Third Folio, which of course has no textual authority. See the discussion in David Berkeley and Donald Eidson, "The Theme of *Henry IV, Part I*," *Shakespeare Quarterly* 19 (1968), 29-31.

[15] Philip Williams, "The Birth and Death of Falstaff Reconsidered," *Shakespeare Quarterly* 8 (1957), 362, argues that during this scene Hal symbolically deposes a father-figure in Falstaff. There are two objections to the contention that Hal is satisfying unconscious parricidal impulses. First, he is playing his father's role in banishing Falstaff.

Hence the obvious symbolism of the episode suggests reconciliation with the values his father represents. Second, there is no substantial evidence in the text that Hal hates his father. Although he does resent his father's disapproval, the tone is one of hurt affection rather than hatred. Mr. Williams shows Henry IV's fears that Hal hates him and wishes for his death, but the passages he cites to show Hal's alleged parricidal impulses (*1HIV*, V.iv.50-56; *2HIV*, IV.v.157-67) overtly support the contrary. Only a strained psychological reading of the lines can yield evidence for his theory.

[16] See *The Fortunes of Falstaff*, pp. 74-75, and Bernard Spivack, "Falstaff and the Psychomachia," *Shakespeare Quarterly* 8 (1957), 449-59.

[17] See Humphreys' introduction, pp. l-liv, and L. C. Knights, *Some Shakespearean Themes* (London, 1959), pp. 51-64.

[18] The close bond between king and kingdom, a commonplace of Renaissance political theory, is suggested by the habit of referring to a king by the name of his land—England, France, or whatever. Erasmus repeats a commonplace when he says, "What the heart is in the body of a living creature, that the prince is in the state" (*The Education of a Christian Prince*, trans. Lester K. Born [New York, 1936], pp. 175-76).

[19] John Lawlor refers allusively to this element in chap. 1, "Appearance and Reality," *The Tragic Sense in Shakespeare* (London, 1960), pp. 17-44.

[20] These plays illustrate the two potentialities of the motif. In *George à Greene* King Edward proves himself a man of his people, in particular when he vails his staff to the shoemakers of Bradford. The emphasis is on kingly humanity. Prince Edward of *Friar Bacon and Friar Bungay*, though attracted to fair Margaret, the lowborn natural aristocrat, overcomes his passion with the magnanimity of royal blood.

[21] The passage may contain a pun on "case," meaning both "state" and "costume or outer garb." At the risk of pushing a metaphor too hard, I would suggest that the second sense implies a common truth: neither Jove, lord of the skies, nor Hal, the future king, destroys his essential being by disguise. Both are "essentially made without seeming so."

[22] Again Erasmus is typical of Renaissance moralists: "The common run of princes zealously avoid the dress and manner of living of the lower classes. Just so should the true prince be removed from the sullied opinions and desires of the common folk" (*The Education of a Christian Prince*, p. 150). Edgar T. Schell, "Prince Hal's Second 'Reformation,'" *Shakespeare Quarterly* 21 (1970), 11-16, sees Hal in this play as reformed from the start but symbolically filling the folkloric role of the Prodigal.

[23] On the relationship of this text to Shakespeare's plays see Humphreys' discussions in *The First Part of King Henry IV*, pp. xxxii-xxxiv, and *The Second Part of King Henry IV*, New Arden Edition (Cambridge, Mass., 1966), pp. xl-xliii.

[24] See the note at IV.v.19 in *The Second Part of King Henry the Fourth*, ed. R. P. Cowl, Arden Edition (London, 1923).

[25] Whatever the legal status of Hal's title, Shakespeare avoids entangling him in his father's guilt. Hugh Dickinson, "The Reformation of Prince Hal," *Shakespeare Quarterly*, 12 (1961), 36-46, esp. 38-39, discusses this, though he minimizes Henry's own guilt further than seems justified.

[26] On the imagery of Cain see Ronald Berman, "The Nature of Guilt in the Henry IV Plays," *Shakespeare Studies* 1 (1965), 20-21.

[27] A. R. Humphreys defends John from this charge in "Shakespeare's Political Justice in *Richard II* and *Henry IV*," *Stratford Papers on Shakespeare*, ed. B. W. Jackson (Toronto, 1965), pp. 46-47.

[28] Humphreys' note at III.ii.128-31 interprets the passage "so the son the mother bears is a likeness cast by the father—but often only the dimmest copy, with little of the paternal substance." But surely Shaaber's note in the New Variorum (at 133-6) is more accurate: "The point of all this punning is plain enough: Falstaff is casting aspersions on Shadow's paternity."

[29] Bernard Spivack, *Shakespeare and the Allegory of Evil* (New York, 1958), makes this distinction.

[30] To make him a Saturn to Hal's Jove, as does Philip Williams, "The Birth and Death of Falstaff Reconsidered," p. 365, is clever and not untrue to the ritualistic emphasis that Shakespeare puts on the rejection scene. However, the association of Saturn with the Golden Age and hence utopian disorder is more relevant than any suggestion of symbolic parricide. For an interesting comparison between Falstaff's decline and Henry IV's, see S. C. Sen Gupta, *Shakespeare's Historical Plays* (London, 1964), pp. 133-34.

[31] As Humphreys' note at V.v.73 points out, critics have read this line in many different ways, but his interpretation, which I follow, is most natural in view of Falstaff's next speech.

[32] A. C. Bradley's classical essay in the *Oxford Lectures on Poetry* has had many followers, two of the most cogent being C. L. Barber, *Shakespeare's Festive Comedy* (Princeton, N.J., 1959), chap. 8, and Jonas A. Barish, "The Turning Away of Prince Hal," *Shakespeare Studies* 1 (1965), 9-17.

[33] Cf. J. I. M. Stewart, *Character and Motive in Shakespeare* (London, 1949), pp. 111-44.

[34] See *Shakespeare from Richard II to Henry V*, chaps. 3 and 4.

Chapter VII

HENRY V

AMONG the history plays, *Henry V* is something of a paradox. It is good without being great, and that is not at all what one would predict following the Henry IV plays. One might expect to see the triumph of Shakespeare's historical vision, the capstone of his second tetralogy, with the ideal king appearing in action against France, England's traditional enemy. Or one would not have been surprised by a daring failure, a play that starts off in a new direction with only partial success, like *Measure for Measure*. Some critics, including Derek Traversi,[1] have seen just such experimentation in *Henry V;* but the foreshadowings of a new Shakespeare are of the faintest even in his account. Besides, *Henry V* is preeminently a successful play; significantly, it has produced one of the best of the Shakespearian films, Sir Laurence Olivier's spectacle.

Clearly *Henry V* is the last of Shakespeare's series of history plays in the 1590s. One can with some confidence date it in the spring or summer of 1599, though it is possible that there was an earlier form or even that it was later revised.[2] In this last of the series, Shakespeare turns to epic drama in order to glorify his ideal king, Henry V, a national hero of legendary proportions and the product of Hal's education in the Henry IV plays.[3] Since Renaissance epic is not characteristically strong in dramatic power, there is peril in such handling. Both the idealized type-characters and the high decorum of language could cripple the stageworthiness of the play. In particular, overemphasis on Shakespeare's lofty manner could have brought back much of the stiffness of the first tetralogy as he tried to duplicate in dramatic verse the stateliness and pictorial richness of *The Faerie Queene* and Chapman's Homer. Such a play might have been all too like *Richard III* without the villain.

However, Shakespeare is too professional a dramatist to leave his hero merely a stiff epic figure. Once again he explores the man behind the public role, the kind of study that yields such rich results in the Henry IV plays. What is difficult to explain is why this approach is less rewarding in *Henry V* than in the two previous plays. Somehow the two sides of this king, public and private, exist parallel to each other but without much interaction. We see a Henry V who relaxes as a man among men, but when he takes on his regal authority, it is as though in gathering his robes about him he becomes a different person. Only in IV.i, perhaps the finest scene in the play, does Henry seem to be trying to define himself, to find some reconciliation of these two sides, as Henry IV and Prince Hal are constantly doing. As a result Henry V does not really seem like Hal grown older. The pressure of Hal's questing intellect is for the most part absent in this confident monarch, and so his intelligence is not so dramatically convincing. Hal is equal to Falstaff's wit—in a sense more than equal, for he can spar with the knight while holding part of himself in reserve. He is not subdued to the quality of his environment, whether in the tavern or on the battlefield at Shrewsbury.

Henry never faces an antagonist of Falstaff's brilliance, and he shows Hal's intellectual detachment only occasionally. Thus he is harder to see apart from the moral ambiguities of his environment. In I.ii he listens to his counselors' advice and makes his decision to invade France, but Shakespeare does little to suggest the thought processes by which he does so. Hence one is left wondering about his motives. Is he a noble patriot being duped by the clergy with their interested motive in supporting a French war? Is he unconcerned with the moral issue of his title as long as it is plausible, since what he wants is a war to unify the English after their long civil strife? Or does he allow for the clergy's bias even while being genuinely concerned with the validity of his title? Though Shakespeare may well have intended the last of these possibilities, one wishes that he had dramatized it more clearly. Perhaps he was overwhelmed by a sense of pervasive evil and corruption in even the noblest undertaking when he wrote *Henry V*. Hence he could not afford to make his king quite so aware of unpleasant reality as Hal is and still have him a patriotic man of action. If so, there is only a short step from this epic-comic history to the tragedy of Brutus, who can be moral only at the cost of willful blindness. (Shakespeare probably wrote *Julius Caesar* at about this time.)

Through most of the play we perceive King Henry

V much more clearly than Harry LeRoy. This unresolved public-private duality spreads out from him to affect the whole play, including the use of the family. Throughout, the family is prominent as a public symbol. Although rhetorical allusions to the family are characteristic of all the history plays, *Henry V* relies more on this device than any other play since the first tetralogy. Woven into the public speeches of the English and French leaders are the traditional themes: the inheritance of virtue, the family as a symbol of unity, and political disorder as a threat to the family. Henry's reliance on his brothers' counsel and support is appropriate to his position as the leader of a unified and vigorous nation. The ideal king depends on his family, not on favorites, and Henry follows his father's advice in doing this (*2 Henry IV*, IV.iv.20-48).

Likewise *Henry V* progresses toward a marriage that both effects and symbolizes union (a momentary one) between the two ancient rivals, France and England. Queen Isabel makes this symbolism explicit at the end of the play:

> God, the best maker of all marriages,
> Combine your hearts in one, your realms in one!
> As man and wife, being two, are one in love,
> So be there 'twixt your kingdoms such a spousal
> That never may ill office, or fell jealousy,
> Which troubles oft the bed of blessed marriage,
> Thrust in between the paction of these kingdoms,
> To make divorce of their incorporate league.
>
> (V.ii.377-84)

This is a formal speech in the old vein, based on the system of correspondences. But this speech has the effect of gratuitous embroidery after the lively comedy of the wooing scene and the cynical realism of the negotiations. Whereas *Richard III* points with solemn inevitability toward the marriage that unites the two warring houses, *Henry V* modulates from a military victory to a playful courtship that suddenly turns out to have symbolic significance.

Similarly, the few episodes of family life in the comic plot lack any thematic connection with the serious plot, unlike the Henry IV plays. Even if one reads *Henry V* as a satire on militarism and hence emphasizes the parodic side of the comic plot,[4] it remains all too directionless and only partly relevant. Pistol arrives onstage in II.i as a bridegroom and promptly engages in a thrasonical quarrel with Nym, a rejected suitor. Their squabbles begin a burlesque of soldierly heroism that runs through the comic episodes, but Shakespeare makes no attempt to parody Henry V's marriage in advance as he had parodied the interview between Hal and his father in *1 Henry IV*.

Perhaps the lack of organic connection comes from the absence of a character like Prince Hal to mediate between the comic and serious plots. A Henry V who can comment without emotion or even wit on Bardolph's execution has lost touch with Falstaff's world, whether or not he finds some community with the tidier low life of Williams and the other common soldiers. Still, though the role of the family may be simpler and less developed than in the Henry IV plays, it is of genuine significance both in general and specifically in developing Henry's character.

One of the Renaissance doctrines on which Shakespeare relies in *Henry V* is moral inheritance. The English and the French agree that breeding should reveal itself in courage and military skill, but the French are puzzled to explain the tenacity of these "Norman bastards" (III.v.10). The Dauphin puts their attitude with vigorous contempt:

> O Dieu vivant! shall a few sprays of us,
> The emptying of our fathers' luxury,
> Our scions, put in wild and savage stock,
> Spirt up so suddenly into the clouds,
> And overlook their grafters?
>
> (III.v.5-9)

In this commonplace imagery even his association of birth with growing plants is traditional. Both son and father have to admit the inbred strength and courage of the English. Weightier because less flippant than this speech is the French king's fearful awareness that Henry descends from Edward III, the victor of Crécy. The grandiloquent mouthings of the French nobles express their decadence and their unwilling admiration for English valor and tenacity. In spite of themselves they praise the breeding of these "mastiffs in robustious and rough coming on" (III.vii.148).

Meanwhile the English proclaim their duty to uphold a noble heritage. The point at issue is whether Henry has a better title to the French crown than its present holder. For all Shakespeare's consciousness of the mixed motives that lead men to war, there seems to be no doubt in the play that the English title to France is valid. The French themselves never question it, and the extraordinary triumph at Agincourt is a sign of God's support for the righteous claims of a united England. However, Shakespeare does raise the question of Henry's title to his own crown, vaguely at first in the conspiracy scene and then explicitly in the king's prayer the night before Agincourt. Even though the English heritage is superior in law and virtue to the French, it has within it a flaw that will lead to the collapse of order and civil war, "Which oft our stage hath shown" (Closing Chorus, 13). The warrior son that Henry and Katherine are to breed is the weakling Henry VI. Nonetheless, the primary contrast is between degenerate chivalry in the French and hereditary valor in the English under their warrior king.

In its rhetoric *Henry V* derives England's glory from its mighty heritage. All of Henry's counselors incite him by means of this heritage when he nears the decision to invade France. In words that foreshadow the French king's reference to Edward III, the Archbishop of Canterbury caps an appeal to Henry's forebears with a picture of that king smiling while his son defeats the French with only half the English forces. The Bishop of Ely and the Duke of Exeter are quick to second this appeal to the warrior blood in Henry's veins. The doctrines of inheritance are woven into Henry's own speech as well. In his grief at the betrayal by Lord Scroop, he includes with Scroop's apparent virtues the noble birth that should have guaranteed them.

As a warrior rallying his troops Henry places special

emphasis on the doctrine of inherited virtue. At Harfleur the climax of his speech is a reminder of his men's
heroic ancestry, first to the nobles and then to the common soldiers:

> On, on, you noblest English!
> Whose blood is fet from fathers of war-proof;
> Fathers that, like so many Alexanders,
> Have in these parts from morn till even fought,
> And sheath'd their swords for lack of argument.
> Dishonour not your mothers; now attest
> That those whom you call'd fathers did beget you.
> Be copy now to men of grosser blood,
> And teach them how to war. And you, good yeomen,
> Whose limbs were made in England, show us here
> The mettle of your pasture; let us swear
> That you are worth your breeding; which I doubt not;
> For there is none of you so mean and base
> That hath not noble lustre in your eyes.
>
> (III.i.17-30)

If Traversi is right in finding unconscious irony suggested by the language just before this, a powerful suggestion that war is unnatural to man,[5] this passage is a
curious reversal. Here the warrior is a natural product
of his birth. Surely this effect is where the primary emphasis of the speech, and the play, lies. If the appeal to
inheritance in Henry's oration has a leanness and vigor
beyond Shakespeare's early style, still it is traditional
in content and in its abstractness of phrasing.

Related to the doctrine of inheritance is the conception of patriotic unity, symbolized by the bonds of family, as a precondition of political and military success.

When Henry makes a decision, he gives due consideration to the counsels of his brothers and uncle, while in
the French court the king engages in unseemly and
fruitless squabbles with his son. The movement toward
temporary harmony at the end is decorated by the two
kings' constant references to each other as "brother
France" and "brother England." This rhetoric of diplomacy is entirely hollow, as is clear from the fact that
Charles invokes the bonds of kinship while agreeing to
disinherit his son so that he may keep the throne during his lifetime, just as Henry VI does. Henry V never
pretends to take this diplomatic rhetoric seriously. All
through Act V he shows a playfulness that reminds one
of Faulconbridge laughing at the false language of
diplomacy. Even the French king catches this spirit
long enough to exchange hard-headed appraisals of the
bargaining under the veil of a joke about virginity.

Such formal language need not be a cloak for the
realities of power politics, however. After the moving
revelation in IV.i of his personal affection for his men,
Henry's celebrated lines at Agincourt ring true:

> We few, we happy few, we band of brothers;
> For he to-day that sheds his blood with me
> Shall be my brother; be he ne'er so vile
> This day shall gentle his condition.
>
> (IV.iii.60-63)

Shedding blood together becomes a figurative union of
bloods. Under such a king the terrible chain of hereditary enmity that has bound England is for the moment
broken.

Facing the task of a righteous war, England draws together like one family. There are both truth and irony in the traitor Grey's words:

> Those that were your father's enemies
> Have steep'd their galls in honey, and do serve you
> With hearts create of duty and of zeal.
>
> (II.ii.29-31)

The treachery by Grey and his companions is not enough to prevent the triumph at Agincourt, though it foreshadows developments that will eventually lose the fruits of victory.[6] The chorus uses the language of correspondences to describe this imperfect unity:

> O England! model to thy inward greatness,
> Like little body with a mighty heart,
> What might'st thou do, that honour would thee do,
> Were all thy children kind and natural!
>
> (Chorus to Act II, 16-19)

In the happy ending of victory in battle and a marriage that combines love and political union, we have only a vague consciousness that there will be unnatural, "kindless" disorder in the family of England, that this precarious unity will collapse.

Nearly as prominent as these two themes is a darker use of the family to express the horrors of war. In the first tetralogy civil war destroys not only love and family loyalty but also wives and children, innocent victims of the conflict. If *Henry V* glorifies the victory at Agincourt, it does so without concealing any of the violence and corruption that taint the English triumph. In contrast with the jesting Dauphin, Henry is determined to assure the justice of his cause before pursuing it into battle because he knows the evils that he will unleash, even on the innocent. At the French court Exeter proclaims Henry's guiltlessness in the war:

> on your head
> Turning the widow's tears, the orphans' cries,
> The dead men's blood, the prived maidens' groans.
> For husbands, fathers, and betrothed lovers,
> That shall be swallow'd in this controversy.[7]
> (II.iv.105-109)

Though Shakespeare may well be paraphrasing Hall,[8] the sentiments are an Elizabethan commonplace. He gives a striking visual quality to another such passage when Henry warns the citizens of Harfleur that continued resistance will expose them and their families to violence. Although this theme does not go beyond the language to permeate the dramatic structure as the other two do and as it did in the plays of civil war, it is still an important part of the imagery of *Henry V*.

Insofar as the family theme goes beyond this essentially public and traditional handling, it does so through Henry himself. Because he is in part an epic figure, the ideal king and warrior, the public language of the family with all its severe dignity is appropriate to him. After all, he represents in the state the moral values that the family stands for in private life. But if Henry is an epic hero, he has more in common with Odysseus than with Achilles. He is the balanced hero, the prudent man, and his story moves toward reconciliation and marriage rather than toward tragedy. Such a hero can be more at his ease than his sterner counterpart, and he is seen in a broader environment, one that includes his personal relationships. Tamburlaine, the Achilles of the English stage, cannot stoop to prose comedy or to wandering among his men in disguise; he is too unitary a character for either. At least in flashes Henry shows a broader, more Odyssean nature.

What is most effectively human about Henry is his desire for companionship. He refuses to accept the isolation involved in royalty. When he does for a moment break through the forms of his office, in the comradeship of battle or in wooing Katherine, he shows a gaiety reminiscent of Prince Hal escaped from the court. When something makes him newly conscious of his isolation, his spirits fall. This side of him is hidden during the formal ceremonies of Act I, but even in his public reproof of the treacherous Scroop something of his personal feeling comes through. He voices the grief of betrayed friendship, a powerful theme in many of the plays and sonnets. As Henry goes to France, he seems entirely alone, there being no hint that he is personally close to any of his brothers.[9]

In the communal effort that leads to Agincourt, he finds the contact with other men that he desires. His spirits rise as the battle nears, especially during the previous night. Although the companionship that he finds is mostly that of brothers in arms rather than actual kin, the family does play some part in the language of IV.i, and in the first few lines he appears among his blood brothers. Now they talk without the solemn formality of the scene in the English court. Henry's moralizing is playful as he shuffles off his kingly distance, first with them and then with the men while he wanders around the camp. Episodes involving the king in disguise are a favorite device of Elizabethan drama, in part because they emphasize his humanity and community with the people. Thus Henry whimsically identifies himself to Pistol as a kinsman to Fluellen, that embodiment of the commonplace virtues.

Henry's debate with the common soldiers implicitly defines the king's similarities and differences from other men. They talk of the king as a man with fears and hopes like theirs, and the disguised Henry is one of them both in physical presence and in manner. The point at issue is how far he is differentiated by his office, especially by responsibility for the individual fates of his soldiers. Both Williams and he think of the family in their dispute. Williams recalls with graphic literalness the effects of war on widows and children, and Henry argues by analogy to a father and son: "So, if a son that is by his father sent about merchandise do sinfully miscarry upon the sea, the imputation of his wickedness, by your rule, should be imposed upon his father that sent him" (IV.i.150-53). Here the fatherhood of the king, a traditional figure of speech, implies what Henry himself illustrates, the combination of authority and personal affection in an ideal king. One thinks of the autocratic Elizabeth and her love for her countrymen. During a scene in which Henry escapes from his formal role, Shakespeare gives these stock references to the family a new immediacy. Henry and Williams argue in the same terms because they are men with the same concerns and values, yet this sameness can emerge only because the king is disguised.

In his soliloquy on ceremony and his prayer, Henry's isolation becomes all the more poignant because for a moment he has been just a man among men. He is left to himself with the responsibilities of kingship and his father's guilt. As king and father to all England, he has to be inhumanly strong and wise; alone before the God whose magistrate he is, he must bear the responsibility that ordinary men escape.

Henry's gaiety and sense of community return with the rising sun. The experience of the past night colors his words to his companions. The high rhetoric of Harfleur mixes with the plain manliness of phrases like "Good God! why should they mock poor fellows thus?" (IV.iii.92). In this way a bridge is made between the formal king of I.ii and the lusty wooer, the plain-speaking man, of V.ii. Henry V is both man and king; his royalty is personal virtue expanded to the larger sphere of public affairs. If this bridge between the private and public man is not so strong as in the Henry IV plays, if it is fully apparent in only one scene, still it is there as an indication of the relationship between man and office.

In the courtship itself we see the man Henry clearly enough, but Shakespeare makes little effort to show the epic king. Johnson remarks discontentedly, "I know not why Shakespeare now gives the king nearly such a character as he made him formerly ridicule in Percy."[10] That is not quite fair, since presumably Henry is playing a part out of sheer exuberance. In one way like Richard III, he exults in the strength that lets him win a lady's love under the most adverse circumstances. Still Johnson's discontent is justified. Ingratiating though the scene may be, it is not really a part of the epic story. Henry plays the farmer seeking a wife, and the game sheds little light on the nature of kingship and on the precarious union between France and England. Hence the ending with its use of the coming marriage as a symbol seems perfunctory, neither triumphant nor effectively ironic.

The excellence of *Henry V* has little to do with the family, partly because Henry's isolation, unlike that of the two Richards, has no moral significance. Despite its traditional role in the language, the family has no broader dramatic role. *Henry V* carries out the pattern of making the family an echo of political themes, but it does not deepen this function.

---

[1] *Shakespeare from Richard II to Henry V* (London, 1957), chap. 5.

[2] The firmest evidence for its date is in the Chorus to Act V (29-34). The lines seem to allude to the expedition against the Irish in 1599, which the Earl of Essex led. Warren D. Smith, "The Henry V Choruses in the First Folio," *JEGP* 53 (1954), 38-57, argues that the allusion is to Mountjoy's campaigns between 1600 and 1603 and that the choruses are a later addition. Most scholars disagree, and Robert Adger Law answers his argument in detail in "The Choruses in *Henry the Fifth*," University of Texas *Studies in English* 35 (1956), 11-21. Among those who argue for an earlier form of the play is J. H. Walter in " 'With Sir John in It,' " *Modern Language Review* 41 (1946), 237-45, and in his New Arden Edition (London, 1954).

[3] Cf. Albert H. Tolman, "The Epic Character of 'Henry V,' " *Falstaff and Other Shakespearean Topics* (New York, 1925), pp. 53-64, and *King Henry V*, ed. Walter, pp. xiv-xxxiv.

[4] For this view see Gerald Gould, "A New Reading of *Henry V*," *English Review* 29 (1919), 42-55, and Harold C. Goddard, *The Meaning of Shakespeare* (Chicago, 1951), pp. 215-68.

[5] Traversi, pp. 181-82.

[6] Shakespeare does not refer to the historical fact that this conspiracy grew out of Henry's questionable title. Whether or not the audience might infer such a motive from Cambridge's cryptic speech at II.ii.155-57, Shakespeare is careful to keep this issue subordinate in a play of foreign wars.

[7] Although the Folio text is ambiguous, Walter's reading "widow's" in line 106 is presumably a misprint for "widows'," since the context demands a series of plurals with "widows'" to match "husbands."

[8] See Walter's note at II.iv.106-9.

[9] Shakespeare does not develop the fondness for Clarence suggested by Henry IV's words (*2HIV*, IV.iv.20-48).

[10] Quoted in *King Henry V*, ed. John Dover Wilson, New Cambridge Shakespeare (Cambridge. Eng., 1947), p. xlii.

Chapter VIII

CONCLUSION

THE family is so basic a human institution that in almost any play or group of plays it has an important role. Shakespeare's history plays are primarily concerned with the public life of his nation, the terrible hundred years of civil strife and wars against the French that haunted the imagination of Elizabethan England and that earlier time of crisis in the reign of King John. His plays express the deepest and most widespread feelings of his countrymen. To them political matters were not of merely theoretical concern; they dreaded the return of a chaos that they knew would involve them and their families in untold suffering. In our age we have trouble responding to or even understanding the *eros* that Elizabethans felt toward their autocratic queen. The principles of order and succession are abstractions, but in the Elizabethans they evoked the most intensely personal feeling.

No man could avoid showing the family in history plays since kings and princes are necessarily fathers and sons, husbands and brothers. But Shakespeare's special contribution is to make the language and episodes of family life relevant to the political themes of

241

the plays. In a kind of drama shaped by Tudor political ideas, Shakespeare makes the family a microcosm of the state and an echo of its values. Marriage and the relationship of father and son, brother and brother, the noble and his house—these are the stuff of a personal drama. He relies on them to give immediacy to his panoramic views of the rise and fall of kings and kingdoms. Ready to his hand is a tradition of seeing in the family a symbol of the state, part of the Elizabethan habit of finding correspondences among all levels of existence. Hence there are traces of the family used similarly in other history plays of the period as well as in the chronicles, moral tracts, and even official pronouncements like the Homilies. But Shakespeare goes beyond his fellows by turning this use of the family into a formal principle, an important part of the whole structure of the plays.

His most conventional use of the family is in the images of family life that permeate the language of the plays. For all the growth of his poetic technique during the 1590s, in *Henry V* he is still inclined to make his references to family relationships abstract and rhetorical. The power of such utterances can be great. Henry V evokes the brutality of war with remarkable clarity when he warns the citizens of Harfleur of the violence facing them, the rape of their daughters and the murder of their infants and aged fathers. But neither the abstract content nor the formal syntax of such passages has changed greatly since Bedford's grotesque description in *1 Henry VI* of the chaos to follow Henry V's death:

CONCLUSION

When at their mothers' moist eyes babes shall suck,
Our isle be made a nourish of salt tears,
And none but women left to wail the dead.

(I.i.49-51)

All the plays are full of generalized references to the doctrine of moral inheritance, to loyalty and order in the family, and to the impact of political order and disorder on the family. At their best these can be striking, and their frequency gives them cumulative effect over the whole span of history plays. Most important, they provide an undercurrent that complements more extensive uses of the family.

Closely related to this poetic technique is the emblematic episode or mirror-scene.[1] In it one of the stock images, such as a father and son's estrangement through political strife, is given fuller dramatic expression in a brief action more or less detachable from the plot of the play. These scenes are simplest and most obvious in the early plays. Henry VI looks on at the battle of Towton in *3 Henry VI* while a father discovers that he has killed his son and a son that he has killed his father. Here a weak monarch watches helplessly as the horrors of civil disorder pass from public to private life. Though the first tetralogy is full of such effects, Shakespeare may have grown tired of their comparative simplicity. In *Richard II* he dissipates the emblematic significance of York's denunciation of his treacherous son by tinging the scenes with savage comedy.

In the later plays such episodes are more a part of their dramatic context and less marked by a heightened, artificial style. Much less formal than the emblematic scenes of the Henry VI plays are those in *1 Henry IV* in which the domestic happiness of the conspirators, especially Hotspur and his wife, provides ironic contrast with the national upheaval they are bringing about. The effect is all the richer for being less conspicuous, more appropriate to the overall tone and dramatic structure.

But these uses of the family are essentially figurative; they are not part of the central dramatic action as it expresses the characters and fates of the main agents in the historical narrative. Acting or refusing to act, men produce historical events, and the character that governs their political behavior reveals itself as well in their domestic lives. One frequent pattern of these plays is that the man and the statesman overlap, that virtues in the one are virtues in the other. Henry VI fails as king and husband; Henry V is victorious at Agincourt and in wooing Katherine.

If that kind of parallel defines the pattern of the Henry VI plays, the dramatic technique is more complicated from *Richard II* on. The principle of ethical similarity still holds, but Shakespeare turns part of his attention to other relationships between public and private life. As he comes to focus on men striving and failing or succeeding in their effort to be good kings, he explores the special pressure that being a king puts on the man. As a result the two realms—public and domestic—are no longer separate. In growing up and coming to terms with his father, Hal learns to be a king, and his personal development is made especially difficult by his position as heir apparent and by his father's questionable title.

CONCLUSION

Richard III culminates Shakespeare's first experiments with the history play. The three *Henry VI* plays are in a sense stepping-stones toward its achievement, though that should not obscure their independent merit. The chronicles gave Shakespeare a large amount of varied material, and the orthodox view of history gave him a theme and a dramatic pattern. In the scarcity of firm knowledge about the theater of the 1580s and 1590s, we can only guess how much he learned from other men; but it is apparent that two strands in dramatic tradition offered some of the techniques that he needed: the largely native morality play and the imported Senecan tragedy. Just as Sackville and Norton drew on them for *Gorboduc,* so Shakespeare with his immensely larger genius used them in dramatizing the England of the civil wars.

There is some plausibility in reducing the plays to one formula or the other.[2] But if one argues, for example, that the heroine of *1 Henry VI* is Respublica torn between the virtues led by Talbot and the vices led by Joan, he has let a convenient metaphor get out of control. Although both *Respublica* and *1 Henry VI* deal with England's welfare, they are not very similar in technique. In the same way one oversimplifies Richard III's character in seeing him as Thyestes or Nero, an ordinary villain-king overcome by nemesis. Shakespeare creates a new, synthetic form even while he draws on elements of the older traditions. In *Richard III* the form reaches maturity.

Although the first tetralogy concentrates on public affairs, these two traditions provide a place for the family as a commentary on the political themes. The theme of inheritance is a natural part of Shakespeare's chosen subject, since the succession of the monarchy was the main element of fifteenth-century history in which the Elizabethans saw lessons for their own time. Also central to the history were the great noble houses with their demands for loyalty often conflicting with duty to the king. But even the elements of family life that seem most detached from great public events have an inner connection with them according to the doctrine of correspondences. Elizabethan audiences would notice that Henry VI's wife usurps the mastery in their marriage just as the Duke of York usurps the throne.

Still there are many other correspondences that can and do provide similar parallels; another reason accounts for the special prominence of the family. Politics was a matter of great concern to every man when Spain and the Roman Catholic church threatened England's life and the succession to the throne was in doubt, but even so politics was a mysterious and distant subject to much of Shakespeare's audience in the popular theater. Issues of state came alive for them when he showed their impact on the family. If ten thousand spectators wept to see Talbot die, it must have been in part because they could imagine how a father and son dying together must feel.[3] When Richard III scoffed at his mother's blessing, they were amused and shocked, but they were not puzzled.

Therefore the primary function of the family in these plays is analogical. It shows the value of political order and the consequences of its perversion. There is a line of characters from Joan of Arc through Jack Cade to Richard III, anarchic figures who attack both the state and the family. These three repudiate their parents in one way or another, and both Joan and Richard earn a parental curse. In the same plays an exhibition of love and trust in the family contrasts ironically with the political disorder and typifies the nationwide harmony to be achieved under Henry Tudor. The filial piety of the younger Talbot, Warwick, and Richmond; Alexander Iden's contentment with his idyllic inheritance; the Duchess of York's noble grief at her family's destruction—all these evoke the same values as Richmond's unifying marriage.

Mirror-scenes are useful in bringing to bear the full symbolic weight of the family. In the Henry VI plays they are more or less peripheral, reinforcing themes established elsewhere; but in *Richard III* the episodes involving the wailing women are essential to show the gradually increasing power working against Richard. At first the women seem as ineffectual as Henry VI on the battlefield of Towton, but the mysterious figure Queen Margaret brings the power to curse. Also, as the Duchess of York comes to dominate Anne and Elizabeth, her strength of character helps them to find a moral stance in opposition to Richard. These three women reassert the values of love and family loyalty. They express the moral order of which Richmond is the physical power. These scenes are less simply emblematic than those in the Henry VI plays, more a part of the dramatic whole.

Thus Shakespeare finds an important place for the family in this group of political plays. But since its function is mainly thematic, the tendency is toward abstraction and generalization. The nuances of a personal relationship are largely irrelevant to the broad moral issues that he is dramatizing. Hence he cultivates a style of lofty impressiveness at the cost of immediacy. By the time of *Richard III*, after a period of experimentation, he has chastened the ritual parts of his poetry to a neo-Senecanism that suits these purposes exactly, a style somewhat like those in Samuel Daniel's *Cleopatra* and Ben Jonson's *Sejanus*, though richer and more exuberant than either.

Something is lost to the family by associating it with this severe style, a directness that makes Joan's father come to life in a few lines of *1 Henry VI*. More and more as the tetralogy goes on, this free, realistic idiom is reserved for the villains like Joan, Jack Cade, and Richard III. Their earthy cynicism cuts across the decorum of language in a way that suggests their anarchy even while it gives them a remarkable vitality in evil. Our aesthetic enjoyment of them should not hide the fact that their anarchy is self-destructive. Although they are worthy antagonists of the nemesis that governs these plays, they are finally destroyed. And as nemesis comes more and more to be equated with Providence, they take their place as a part of the overall pattern.

Richard III is a brilliant achievement in its own terms, but it is an idea-centered play. Despite the great vitality of its protagonist, the building-blocks of the play are concepts rather than characters. The play, indeed the whole tetralogy, succeeds because these concepts are woven into a rich and meaningful pattern, one in which even the striking figure of Richard Crookback has his place. Hereafter Shakespeare's dramatic art will take a new turn, but no other Elizabethan play excels *Richard III* in its own mode. There is room for a deeper exploration of the family, but Shakespeare must devise a new form for the history play to admit such exploration and adapt it to a political theme. If a character developed as fully as Richard and having his vitality of language were placed in the family, not isolated from it, a whole new range of potentiality would open up.

King John and *Richard II* include some of Shakespeare's experimentation with the history play. In outline *King John* repeats some of the major themes of *Richard III*. It portrays an efficient usurper who loses control of events when his brutality toward the rightful heir to the throne mobilizes opinion against him. But the rigid moral antitheses of *Richard III* have no place in this play. In spite of a first impression of Machiavellian ability, John is no demon but a weak and vacillating man. Also the motives of idealism and commodity are mixed indiscriminately between his friends and enemies. Somewhere in the past is an ideal England, associated with Richard Coeur-de-Lion's glorious rule, but this present land has lost its legitimacy. Power, ability, and title to the throne are hopelessly fragmented, and it takes years of suffering before Englishmen can work out the salvation of their land through a combination of loyalty and practical sense.

Faulconbridge's words give a choric analysis of this political dilemma, and his position is a symbolic analogue of England's plight. Tainted by bastardy, he is thrust into a moral land of shadows in which every ethical choice is ambiguous. To claim his legal inheritance is to rely on a quirk of the law while denying his real self. To claim his moral inheritance from Richard I is to admit his bastardy, hurt his mother's reputation, and abandon himself to the perils of dependence on courtly favor. Still he chooses easily enough, and Shakespeare makes clear the rightness of his choice and his position in the play as moral commentator. He is the main embodiment of the shrewdness and patriotic fidelity that preserve England for its legitimate king, John's son.

Richard II is another study of a weakly evil king, and it starts the chain of guilt that ends only with Richmond's victory in *Richard III*. Still the pattern of guilt and disorder is overshadowed by interest in Richard's character as he reacts to adversity. Of special importance for the next three histories is the concern with how Richard's official role affects his understanding of himself. Here Shakespeare takes up with new interest the relationship between the public and private man. It is not true, as romantic critics like Yeats argued, that Richard's vices are only political and that he is a creature too spiritual for the dirty work of governing men. His cruelty as a king manifests itself in part by an attack on his own family, and he shows no signs of genuine personal attachment to anyone, even after he is humbled by grief. But the isolation that he himself has chosen is painful to him, especially since it forces him to confront the truth of his fall without any support. His tragedy is that his failure to live up to his royal office destroys him as a man.

Although the family has a part in both plays, in neither is its significance unequivocal. The pathos of

Constance and Arthur or of Gaunt's regret for his son's
banishment is in the vein of the first tetralogy, but they
are isolated events in their plays, not part of a coherent
pattern that mobilizes spiritual force against enemies of
the family and political order. In these two plays there
is something nostalgic and unreal about the values of
the family, and so a character like York is slightly ab-
surd in his rigid probity. When he defends Bolingbroke's inheritance before Richard and especially when
he offers his son's life out of loyalty to Bolingbroke,
now the new king, York's virtue is anachronistic. Its
practical use is doubtful since it has no consequences
in the action. In both plays the references to the family
and episodes of family life often have a new poetic richness and power, but they are not integral to the dramatic structure. The antithesis of order and chaos, love
and ambition, no longer gives shape to the action and
symbolic meaning to the family.

In the Henry IV plays Shakespeare finds a pattern
that allows him to relate the family to the state without
reverting to the simpler parallels of the first tetralogy.
All the themes from Tudor orthodoxy are still there.
Shakespeare constantly implies the need for order and
for the extension of personal virtues like love and loyalty to the public realm. But in turning to a new theme,
the education of a prince, he adapts a popular dramatic
form built on the parable of the Prodigal Son. Christ's
parable uses family life as a symbol of man's relationship to God, and so it is easily adapted to the multiple
levels of Shakespeare's concern. Hal is a son who
breaks away from his father but finally returns to take
his place in the family. At the same time he is a prince

who gains insight into his land by escaping the court and seeing the taverns and back roads. This escape involves the peril of weakening his position as heir to the throne, but on his return Hal takes up his heritage and even brings new strength to it. In his reconciliation with his father the king, he reaffirms his commitment to the principle of order. After his coronation he promises the man who has dared to judge even him with justice, "You shall be as a father to my youth" (*2 Henry IV*, V.ii.118).

Of all the characters in the two Henry IV plays, only Hal chooses the values of the family with complete integrity and comprehension of the issues involved. Some of the others offer verbal tribute, using the formal language of the first tetralogy, but their actions belie their commitment. Thus the Percies demonstrate their unworthiness for rule by their disloyalty to one another. Only Hotspur is unwavering in his fidelity to the common cause, and he keeps his integrity by a thorough blindness to his partners' motives. His simple chivalric code, both admirable and slightly comic, is all that holds the Percy rebellion together. When his father betrays him and lets him take the field at Shrewsbury against hopeless odds, his death ends the Percies' effective power. Hal, reconciled with Henry IV, kills Hotspur in a single combat that acts out their duel for moral supremacy.

Opposite Hotspur, Falstaff has the clown's prerogative of parodying everything in the serious plot, including the family themes. He is the old generation masquerading as youth, and he pretends to be a father to Hal who must pass on to him the code of moral inheritance. The inheritance he offers is the code of Puritan highwaymen. To the extent that Falstaff is joking, Hal can play his game; but there is a serious claim to influence and favor in the knight's manner that Hal must finally reject. Liberal education though his friendship is, Falstaff is also a tempter toward anarchy. Hal's ironic detachment allows him to enjoy Falstaff without succumbing to his influence. The fat knight is a father to Hal's youthful spirits, but not to his moral commitments.

Central to Hal's growth toward fitness for the monarchy are the two confrontations with his father—especially the second, when the old king is dying. Here Shakespeare dramatizes Hal's attainment of personal maturity and with it his acceptance of his public role. As Henry talks with his son, his clarity of vision is dimmed by age, sickness, and the pressure of maintaining himself on a doubtful throne; but his selfless concern with England's future shows him at his best. For all his guilt, Henry has both shrewdness and virtue for his son to inherit. Hal acts with propriety and affection to calm his father's doubts, but the intensity of his feeling suggests that the estrangement has been real enough. He has sought to escape the court in part because he knows the strain of being in authority. Hence he takes the crown from his father's bed with full consciousness of its burdens. Ironically, Henry completely misunderstands Hal's act, but his misunderstanding leads to the confrontation that clears the air between them. Henry can die in confidence that his son will carry on the Lancastrian heritage. He even hopes that

Hal has escaped the guilt of Richard's deposition and death.

The two Henry IV plays have a unity more like the *Faerie Queene* than the *Aeneid*. They form coherent patterns through a network of themes that weave in and out of a complex narrative, one that lacks even a protagonist as dominant as either of the two Richards. Hal's education occupies a central position between the political and comic plots, but it does not monopolize the interest of the plays. And even that theme allows for an extraordinary richness and complexity of development. Shown as it is in the Prodigal Son pattern, it includes psychological, political, and even religious meanings. It is as though Shakespeare turned to the other potentiality of correspondences so as to find multiple levels of meaning in one set of events.

The central concern of the Henry IV plays is still political, but the political issues are seen in a broader and more human way than in the first tetralogy. The abstractions of Tudor orthodoxy are less important than the problem of how a man can live up to his divinely appointed role. Shakespeare has given these doctrines a new depth by showing the human meaning of the great abstractions: order, majesty, patriotism, inherited nobility.

In *Henry V* Shakespeare undertakes to set forth an orderly state under an ideal king and to show that state conquering a mighty rival by the sheer impact of its virtue. Henry V is able to draw England together into a harmony and vigor that the French cannot rival. Such a theme being central, the family is not a primary concern, at least in the full development of the Henry IV plays. However, Shakespeare uses it as a public symbol, a touchstone by which to test the comparative merit of the English and the French, including their governors. Henry embodies the private virtues as well as the public, and the disorderly squabbles of the French king and the Dauphin illustrate the decay of the French commonweal.

Still *Henry V* is more than a political pageant. Henry himself is not just another Talbot because Shakespeare no longer allows his hero to have a merely public existence. However, it is through comradeship in arms rather than family life that we see most deeply into Henry's personal feelings. Much of his behavior is formal and public; only on the night before Agincourt does he reveal himself with the fullness of Shakespeare's mature craft. Powerful though that scene is and for all the exhilaration of the battle scenes, *Henry V* is a less interesting play than its two historical predecessors. Perhaps one reason is its return to a simpler and more formal way of using the family.

One conclusion should be apparent if this analysis is valid: the family as part of man's personal life is not opposed to what is needed for success in public affairs. It is true that a king must lose the sense of personal contact with others which private men can feel and that Shakespeare finds a deep pathos in this loss. However, the family can serve as an analogy to the state precisely because their ethics are parallel. It is the school of political nobility and skill, and it suffers when the governors of the commonwealth lack virtue. Because it and the state are parts of a larger organism, their healths are interdependent. This doctrine allows

Shakespeare to develop a dramatic technique that modulates between the public and private worlds. His plays can have both scope and unity because he sees a larger unity in the nature to which he holds up the mirror. But the metaphysic of correspondences does not offer a dramatic technique fully developed for his use. His growth as a craftsman during the 1590s is in part an expansion of scope to take in more and more of man's life without losing unity and control. One side of that growth comes through the history plays as he learns to illuminate both the family and the political world by their relation to each other.

[1] For the term and concept see Hereward Price, "Mirror-Scenes in Shakespeare," *Joseph Quincy Adams Memorial Studies,* ed. James G. McManaway et al. ('Washington, D.C., 1948), pp. 101-13.

[2] On occasion E. M. W. Tillyard and Irving Ribner do nearly that. Comparing *Richard III* with the Henry VI plays, Ribner comments, "England continues as a kind of morality hero torn between good and evil forces" (*The English History Play in the Age of Shakespeare* [Princeton, N.J., 1957], p. 118). To call England or Respublica the heroine of the history plays describes their theme accurately enough, but it also makes certain misleading implications about their dramatic structure.

[3] See Thomas Nashe's apparent allusion to the popularity of this scene in *Pierce Pennilesse,* quoted in *The First Part of King Henry VI,* ed. John Dover Wilson, New Cambridge Edition (Cambridge, Eng., 1952), p. xiv.

INDEX

257

INDEX

Emblematic scenes. *See* Family, the: in mirror-scenes

Empson, William, 222

Epic hero, the, 11, 41–42, 225-26, 235–36

Erasmus, 1, 5, 6, 9, 88, 223

Everyman, 16–17

Falstaff, 30, 173–74, 252–53; in *1 Henry IV*, 174–75, 179–83, 192–96; in *2 Henry IV*, 196–97, 198, 199–200, 203, 214–17, 220

Family, the. *See also* Bastardy; Brothers as theme; Fathers and sons; Inheritance; Marriage; Prodigal Son as motif; Virtue, public and private
—as correspondence: in Renaissance literature, 1, 23–28; in Renaissance theory, 4–9; in Shakespeare, 28–30, 241–56; in *Henry VI*, 35–37, 51, 65–67, 85–86; in *Richard III*, 91, 118–19; in *King John*, 126–27, 167–68; in *Richard II*, 149, 166–68; in *Henry IV*, 171–76, 196–97, 217–21; in *Henry V*, 228, 239
—as victim, 23–25, 26–27, 242–43; in *Henry VI*, 23–24, 38–39, 53–54, 67–74, 87, 242–43, 246; in *Richard III*, 93–97, 111–14; in *King John*, 127–28; in *Richard II*, 24, 149–50, 163; in *Henry IV*, 176–77, 212–14; in *Henry V*, 234–35, 237, 242
—in mirror-scenes, 23–39, 40–41, 43–46, 51, 56–57, 68–73, 106–22, 157–58, 243–44, 247

Famous Victories of Henry the Fifth, The, 201, 224

Fathers and sons. See also Inheritance; Prodigal Son as motif
—as characters, 15–16, 18, 25–26; in *Henry VI*, 11–12, 48, 55–56, 73–74, 76–85; in *King John*, 141; in *Richard II*, 150–55, 157–60, 169; in *Henry IV*, 12, 171–

90, 192–96, 197, 201–13, 217, 222–23, 253–54
—in isolated images, 1, 23–27, 54, 66–67, 88, 96–98, 136, 153, 215–16, 237
—in mirror-scenes, 23–24, 43–46, 56–57, 68–73, 157–58, 246

Faulconbridge, 9, 28, 126, 129, 130–31, 137–44, 168, 249–50

Friar Bacon and Briar Bungay (Robert Greene), 199, 223

Gammer Gurton's Needle (W. Stevenson?), 17, 22–23

Gascoigne, George, 22, 44

Gaunt, John of, 153–55, 157–59, 166; as mentioned in *3H6*, 77

George à Greene (Robert Greene?), 199,223

Glass of Government, The (George Gascoigne), 22

Gloucester, Eleanor, duchess of (*2 Henry VI*), 58–59, 60, 87

Gloucester, Eleanor, duchess of (*Richard II*), 154–55

Gloucester, Humphrey, duke of, 51, 52, 54, 58–59, 61, 64, 70, 87, 156

Gorboduc (Sackville and Norton), 10, 13, 16, 23, 158

Greene, Robert, 26, 199, 223

Guazzo Stefano, 7, 79

Hal, Prince, 11–12, 29, 171–74, 218–20, 226–27, 251–54; in *Richard II*, 160; in *1 Henry IV*, 174–88, 191–96, 222–23; in *2 Henry IV*, 196–97, 199–203, 205–11, 215–17, 223. *See also* Henry V.

Hall, Edward, 3, 33, 86–87, 90, 100, 121, 235

Harbage, Alfred (quoted) 12, 222

Henry IV, 29, 171–74; in *1 Henry IV*, 175–79, 183–88, 192–95; in

258

INDEX